WORKBOOK TO ACCOMPANY PRACTICAL STATISTICS FOR EDUCATORS

THIRD EDITION

Ruth Ravid

Elizabeth Oyer

University Press of America,® Inc.
Lanham · Boulder · New York · Toronto · Oxford

Copyright © 2005 by
University Press of America,® Inc.
4501 Forbes Boulevard
Suite 200
Lanham, Maryland 20706
UPA Acquisitions Department (301) 459-3366

PO Box 317
Oxford
OX2 9RU, UK

Library of Congress Control Number: 2005924779
ISBN 0-7618-3224-6 (paperback : alk. ppr.)

TABLE OF CONTENTS

FOREWORD

This workbook accompanies the textbook PRACTICAL STATISTICS FOR EDUCATORS (3rd ed., Ravid, 2005). The main purpose of the workbook is to allow students to review and apply the material presented in the textbook. The chapters and exercises in the workbook correspond to the chapters in the textbook. The workbook includes exercises that require students to recall, comprehend, apply, interpret, analyze, and synthesize information. Various item formats are used, such as multiple-choice, matching, filling-in-the-blanks, short answers, and computation. Answers to each chapter's exercises can be found at the end of the chapter to allow the students to get immediate feedback and confirm their own answers. The answers to some of the exercises include detailed explanations of the correct answers in order to elaborate on the reasons for the correct response.

Because more and more people use statistical software programs to analyze their data, the work book includes only a few exercises that require the use of calculators. The emphasis is on skills that every teacher researcher needs to know: How to select the appropriate statistical test to analyze the data and how to interpret the data calculated by the computer. Supplemental computer exercises that apply the chapter content are at the end of many chapters. The exercises require the use of Microsoft™ Office Excel, version 1998 or later[1]. The data required for the exercises are available for download at http://www.evalsolutions.com/Practical_Statistics/index.htm.

---

[1] Microsoft Office Excel is a registered trademark of Microsoft Corporation. Screen shots are reproduced with the permission of Microsoft Corporation and are not intended to suggest an endorsement of this workbook.

Chapter 1

AN OVERVIEW OF EDUCATIONAL RESEARCH

Circle the <u>correct</u> answer:

1.1 The type of research designed to solve a problem by studying it and implementing a solution to the problem is called **pure/action** research

1.2. The type of research where researchers focus on studying phenomena in their natural context, using multiple and subjective data sources is called **qualitative/quantitative** research.

1.3. In experimental studies, researchers manipulate the **dependent/independent** variable and observe its effect on the **dependent/independent** variable.

1.4. In causal-comparative studies, the independent variable **is/is not** manipulated.

1.5. In experimental studies, unplanned or uncontrolled variables which may affect the outcomes of the studies are called **dependent/extraneous** variables.

1.6. Studies in which extraneous variables are controlled are said to have high **internal/external** validity.

1.7. When the results of the study can be generalized to other settings and populations, the study is considered to have **internal/external** validity.

1.8. In studies where people behave in a way that is different from their normal behavior because they are being observed by the researchers, there may be a threat to the study's **statistical regression/external validity**.

1.9. In most experimental studies, when the groups being compared are formed by randomly assigning people to groups, these groups are considered **more/less** similar to each other compared with the majority of studies where intact groups are being compared.

1.10. In pre-experimental studies, there is usually a **greater/smaller** number of threats to internal validity compared with true experimental studies.

1.11. Experimental and control groups are tested *repeatedly* before and after the intervention in quasi-experimental studies which are called **time-series/counterbalanced** designs.

1.12.   In studies where a counterbalanced design is used, all groups receive all interventions in **the same/a different** order.

1.13.   A-B-A designs are used to study the effect of an intervention on **individuals/groups**.

1.14.   A-B-A designs include **one/two** baseline phase(s) and **one/two** intervention phase(s).

1.15.   Studies designed to measure how children change over time, without the use of any planned intervention, are called **cross-sectional/time-series** studies.

Circle the best answer:

1.16.   The type of research which is aimed at testing theories and applying them to specific situations is called _____

    a.   applied research.
    b.   action research.
    c.   pure research.
    d.   basic research.

1.17.   Research conducted in the lab under a tight control of all variables is called _____

    a.   applied research.
    b.   action research.
    c.   pure research.
    d.   qualitative research.

1.18.   Studies where researchers look for changes in the dependent variable which may happen as a result of manipulating the independent variable are called _____ studies.

    a.   experimental
    b.   ex post facto
    c.   causal-comparative
    d.   qualitative

1.19.   Studies which attempt to establish cause-and-effect relationship are called _____

      a.   qualitative studies.
      b.   descriptive studies.
      c.   experimental studies.
      d.   cross-sectional studies.

1.20.   Uncontrolled events happening outside longer-duration experimental studies which can have an effect on the dependent variable, may pose a threat to the study's internal validity that is called _____

      a.   instrumentation.
      b.   statistical regression.
      c.   testing.
      d.   history.

1.21.   The Solomon Four-Groups design allows researchers to test the effect of the intervention, as well as a threat to internal validity called _____

      a.   maturation.
      b.   testing.
      c.   statistical regression.
      d.   differential selection.

1.22.   Causal-comparative research is also called _____

      a.   pre-experimental research.
      b.   time-series research.
      c.   action research.
      d.   ex-post facto research.

1.23.   Experimental studies where two pre-existing groups are used as experimental and control groups are called _____

      a.   true experimental studies
      b.   cross-sectional studies
      c.   quasi experimental design studies
      d.   A-B-A case studies

1.24.   Studies where groups are tested multiple times before and after the intervention are called _____

   a.   time-series studies
   b.   counterbalanced studies
   c.   Solomon Four Group studies
   d.   one group pretest-posttest studies

1.25.   The target behavior is assessed before and after the intervention in studies employing the _____

   a.   pre-experimental design
   b.   the A-B-A design
   c.   cross-sectional design
   d.   longitudinal design

1.26.   To study how individuals change over time, researchers may conduct _____

   a.   causal-comparative research
   b.   true experimental research
   c.   time-series research
   e.   cross-sectional research

1.27.   Studies where data are collected over two or more points in time for the <u>same</u> people are called _____

   a.   cross-sectional studies
   b.   panel studies
   c.   trend studies
   d.   case studies

1.28.   A study is designed to assess the effect of cooperative learning on the social skills of third-grade students. Twice a day, during free play, observers count the number of positive interactions among the students who are taught using cooperative learning. In this study, the <u>independent</u> variable is the _____

   a.   cooperative learning.
   b.   students' grade level.
   c.   number of positive interactions.
   d.   number of free play periods during the day.

1.29.   A study is designed to assess whether computer training is likely to increase teachers' use of computers in their teaching. Teachers who have participated in a semester-long computer training are observed for three months before and after the training to determine how many hours per week they use computers in their teaching. In this study, the <u>dependent</u> variable is the _____

     a.   semester-long computer training course.
     b.   number of hours per week that teachers use computers in their teaching.
     c.   observers who record computer use in the classrooms.
     d.   three months before and after the study, when teachers are observed.

1.30.   A school psychologist wants to conduct a causal-comparative study to explore the effect of IQ on the self-concept of middle-school students. The psychologist administers a measure of self-concept to a group of 300 students (from grades 6, 7, and 8). The students' IQ scores range from 100-130. In this study, the <u>independent</u> variable is the _____

     a.   school psychologist.
     b.   number of students.
     c.   students' grade level.
     d.   students' IQ scores.

1.31.   The study described in the previous question (about IQ and self-concept) is considered a causal-comparative study because _____

     a.   the dependent variable cannot be manipulated.
     b.   the independent variable cannot be manipulated.
     c.   there are three different grade levels in the study.
     d.   some extraneous variables cannot be controlled in this study.

1.32.   A study is conducted to test two methods to treat depressed teenagers. Seventy children, ages 13-18, diagnosed as depressed, are randomly assigned to the two intervention groups. The two interventions consist of a series of weekly meetings and online chat among the members of each group and their counselors. A measure to assess their level of depression is administered to the study's participants before and after the intervention. The design of the study is:

     a.   true experimental design
     b.   counterbalanced design
     c.   quasi experimental design
     d.   time series

Chapter 1: Answers

(1.1) action;
(1.2) qualitative;
(1.3) independent; dependent;
(1.4) is not;
(1.5) extraneous;
(1.6) internal;
(1.7) external;
(1.8) external validity;
(1.9) more; (<u>Explanation</u>: Groups formed by using random assignment are considered to be more similar to each other compared with groups formed by using any other procedure.)
(1.10) greater; (<u>Explanation</u>: In pre-experimental designs is it more difficult to control variables that may negatively affect the study's internal validity.)
(1.11) time-series; (<u>Explanation</u>: In time-series designs, there is usually only one intervention, and the groups are tested several times before and after each intervention; in counterbalance designs, there are several interventions, but only one testing after each intervention.)
(1.12) a different;
(1.13) individuals;
(1.14) two; one;
(1.15) cross-sectional;
(1.16) a;
(1.17) c;
(1.18) a; (<u>Explanation</u>: In causal-comparative/ex post facto studies and in qualitative research studies, the independent variable is not manipulated at all; it is manipulated only in experimental studies.)
(1.19) c;
(1.20) d;
(1.21) b;
(1.22) d;
(1.23) c;
(1.24) a;
(1.25) b;
(1.26) d;
(1.27) b;
(1.28) a; (<u>Explanation</u>: This is an experimental study, designed to study cause-and-effect relationship. In the study, cooperative learning is the independent variable [the "cause"] and social skills, expressed as the number of positive interactions among the students, are the dependent variable [the "effect"].)
(1.29) b; (<u>Explanation</u>: The outcome measure - the dependent variable - is the teachers' use of computers, expressed as the number of hours per week they use computers in their teaching.)

(1.30) d; (<u>Explanation</u>: We want to test the effect of IQ on self-concept; therefore, the students' IQ is the independent variable - the "cause" - and the students' self-concept scores are the dependent variable – the "effect".)

(1.31) b; (<u>Explanation</u>: This is a causal-comparative study and not an experimental study, because IQ, which is the independent variable, cannot be manipulated.)

(1.32) a; (<u>Explanation</u>: It is a true experimental design, because children are assigned at random to the groups. The design listed in the other three answers do not included groups with random assignment of participants.)

Chapter 2

BASIC CONCEPTS IN STATISTICS

Identify each as a <u>variable</u> or a <u>constant</u>:

2.1.   The <u>number of months</u> in a year.

2.2   The <u>gender</u> of teenage girls in a study designed to investigate their career aspirations.

2.3.   The <u>age</u> when people choose to retire.

2.4.   The <u>ACT scores</u> of the senior class students.

Identify each variable as <u>continuous</u> or <u>discrete</u>:

2.5.   Grade level

2.6.   Age

2.7.   Height

2.8.   Number of children in a family

Identify each as <u>nominal</u>, <u>ordinal</u>, <u>interval</u>, or <u>ratio</u>:

2.9.   The TV channel watched the most on Thursday night in four cities.

2.10.   The percentage of respondents watching each TV program at 8:00pm on Thursday.

2.11.   Ranking of the 5 most important problems in the U.S.A. today.

2.12.   List of ACT scores for the high schools in the county.

2.13.   Classification of students by the state where they were born.

2.14.   The number of residents in six different states.

2.15.   High school rank.

Classify each as <u>descriptive</u> or <u>inferential</u> statistics:

2.16   The mean scores of all third grade classes on a standardized achievement test.

2.17.   The results of the TV ratings as obtained by A.C. Nielsen for 3000 households with the people-meter (the "black box").

2.18   The number of students from single-parent and two-parent families in Lincoln School.

2.19   The blood pressure of a group of volunteers given a new experimental drug to lower blood pressure.

Fill in the blanks:

2.20   The most important characteristic of a good sample is that it is _____ of the population.

2.21.   A study where numerical information about the total population is gathered by including <u>all</u> members of the population is called a _____.

2.22.   The sample's statistics are used to estimate the population's _____.

2.23.   When every 20th person is chosen from a group of 1000 people, we obtain a _____ sample.

2.24.   A hypothesis that predicts that *there is* a difference or relationship between variables or groups is called the _____ hypothesis, and is represented by the symbol H_A or H_1.

2.25.   When means from two groups are compared, the <u>null</u> hypothesis states that the difference between the means is _____.

2.26.   In order to decide whether the null hypothesis should be rejected or retained, the *sample* statistic obtained as a result of the statistical calculations is compared to the appropriate _____, found usually in a table in an appendix in statistics books.

2.27.   In many statistical tests, degrees of freedom (*df*) are calculated by subtracting 1 from _____.

Circle the correct answer:

2.28   A biased sample contains a **random/systematic** error.

2.29   A random sample **is always/may not always be** representative of the population from which it was selected.

2.30.   To analyze data measured on a *nominal* scale, researchers should use **parametric/nonparametric** statistics.

2.31.   The information gained about the sample is used to generalize to the population and to estimate its values in **descriptive/inferential** statistics.

2.32.   Inferential statistics **may/may not** include descriptive statistics, such as the mean.

2.33.   When we predict which mean is going to be higher, our hypothesis is **directional/nondirectional.**

2.34.   If we reject the null hypothesis at $p<.01$, we are **more/less** confident that we made the right decision compared with rejecting the null hypothesis at the $p<.05$ level.

2.35.   When there is a *very small* difference between means obtained on a measure at the end of a study, the null hypothesis is likely to be **rejected/retained**.

2.36.   A low correlation is more likely to be statistically significant when the sample size is **large/small**.

2.37.   When the probability level is set prior to the start of the study, it is represented by the letter **p/alpha (α)**.

2.38.   The error made by researchers who retain a null hypothesis when in fact it should be rejected is called **Type I/Type II** error.

2.39   The hypothesis that always states that the correlation is not significantly different from zero is the **null/alternative** hypothesis.

2.40.   Effect size is used to evaluate the **practical/statistical** significance of the study.

2.41.   When selecting a number of equal-size samples from the same population, the means of the samples are likely to be **the same as/different from** the population mean.

2.42.   The standard error of the means is the standard deviation of the **sample means/population means**.

2.43.   To estimate a population value that is of interest to them, researchers use the **effect size/confidence interval**.

Circle the best answer:

2.44.   Equal distances between the various points on the scale are found in _____.

    a.   a nominal scale
    b.   an ordinal scale
    c.   both nominal and ordinal scales
    d.   both interval and ratio scales

2.45.   Using numbers to represent categories of observations is an example of a(n)_____ scale.

    a.   nominal
    b.   ordinal
    c.   interval
    d.   ratio

2.46.   Equal distances between the various points on the scale, as well as an absolute zero, are found in a(n) ____ scale.

    a.   nominal
    b.   ordinal
    c.   interval
    d.   ratio

2.47.   A sampling procedure where every member of the population has an independent and equal chance of being selected is called a _____ sample.

    a.   systematic
    b.   random
    c.   stratified
    d.   convenience

2.48.   A sample that represents proportionally each segment of the population is a _____ sample.

    a.   random
    b.   systematic
    c.   stratified
    d.   convenient

2.49.   When every 15th person is selected from a population of 2000 people, the obtained sample is a _____ sample.

    a.   stratified
    b.   systematic
    c.   random
    d.   biased

Answers - Chapter 2:

(2.1) Constant; (<u>Explanation</u>: The number of months is always the same: 12);

(2.2) Constant; (<u>Explanation</u>: Since only girls participate, gender does not vary and is a constant.)

(2.3) Variable; (<u>Explanation</u>: Different people choose to retire at different ages.)

(2.4) Variable; (<u>Explanation</u>: The ACT scores of the seniors are likely to differ from each other.)

(2.5) Discrete; (<u>Explanation</u>: Grade levels have increments of whole units only; that is, one cannot be in grade 3.2, for example.)

(2.6) Continuous; (<u>Explanation</u>: There are many small increments between the various ages; for example, between the age of 10 and 11, there can be small increments, such as 10 years and one day, 10 years and 2 days.)

(2.7) Continuous; (<u>Explanation</u>: The same argument as in the example about age above.)

(2.8) Discrete; (<u>Explanation</u>: The number of children is increased in whole units increments; for example, we cannot have 2.4 children in the family, only 1 or 2 or 3, etc.)

(2.9) Nominal; (<u>Explanation</u>: Although the channels are represented by numbers, these numbers are used for identification only and represent categories.)

(2.10) Ratio; (<u>Explanation</u>: Percentages are considered a ratio scale, because "0%" is viewed as a true/absolute zero);

(2.11) Ordinal; (<u>Explanation</u>: By ranking, we are ordering the problems, thereby creating an ordinal scale);

(2.12) Interval; (<u>Explanation</u>: ACT scores, as well as most other test scores, are considered an interval scale.)

(2.13) Nominal; (<u>Explanation</u>: The states are categorical data.)

(2.14) Ratio; (<u>Explanation</u>: The number of residents in each state is likely to be different. For example, we can say that one state has twice as many people as another state.)

(2.15) Ordinal; (<u>Explanation</u>: By ranking observations we create an ordinal scale.)

(2.16) Descriptive; (<u>Explanation</u>: Since *all* the third grade classes are included, the mean is viewed as representing a population, not a sample.)

(2.17) Inferential; (<u>Explanation</u>: The 3000 households are considered a sample that represents the total population of TV viewers.)

(2.18) Descriptive; (<u>Explanation</u>: There is no intention of viewing the school as a sample of some larger population.)

(2.19) Inferential; (<u>Explanation</u>: The volunteers are used as a sample, and their reaction to the drug would be generalized to the general population.)

(2.20) representative;

(2.21) census;

(2.22) parameters;

(2.23) systematic;

(2.24) alternative;

(2.25) zero;

(2.26) critical value;

(2.27) n (the number of people in the group);

(2.28) systematic; (<u>Explanation</u>: *Random* errors are expected when drawing samples from a population, but *systematic* errors in the samples indicate a bias.)

(2.29) may not always be; (<u>Explanation</u>: While a random sample is likely to be representative of the population, if the sample is small [$n<30$], it may not be representative of the population from which it was selected.)

(2.30) nonparametric; (<u>Explanation</u>: To use *parametric* statistics, data have to be measured on an *interval* or *ratio* scale.)

(2.31) inferential; (<u>Explanation</u>: Inferential statistics refer to the use of samples to estimate and make inferences about the population values.)

(2.32) may; (<u>Explanation</u>: Inferential statistics may include descriptive statistics, such as the mean. The two types of statistics are not mutually exclusive.)

(2.33) directional; (<u>Explanation</u>: Directional hypotheses are used when the researcher predicts which mean will be higher or when the researcher predicts the direction of the correlation [positive or negative].)

(2.34) more; (<u>Explanation</u>: A p value of .01 indicate that there is 1% chance that the decision to reject the null hypothesis is the wrong decision, whereas a p value of .05 indicate that the likelihood is 5%. Therefore, rejecting the null hypothesis at $p<.01$ indicates more confidence in the findings than a when rejecting the null hypothesis at $p<.05$.)

(2.35) retained; (<u>Explanation</u>: In studies where there is a small difference between the means, we are more likely to conclude that the difference could have happened purely by chance and therefore we would retain the null hypothesis.)

(2.36) large; (<u>Explanation</u>: When the sample sizes are large, even small correlation coefficients are likely to be statistically significant.)

(2.37) alpha (α); (<u>Explanation</u>: Probability levels stated prior to the start of the study are called alpha, whereas the probability levels used when analyzing the data at the end of the study are called p values.)

(2.38) Type II; (<u>Explanation</u>: Retaining a *false* null hypothesis is referred to as Type II error, while rejecting a *true* null hypothesis is referred to as Type I error.)

(2.39) null; (<u>Explanation</u>: Only null hypotheses always predict that the correlation is zero. Alternative hypotheses may also predict that the correlation is positive or negative or different from zero.)

(2.40) practical; (<u>Explanation</u>: The p value is used to indicate the study's *statistical* significance whereas effect size is used to evaluate the *practical* significance of the results.)

(2.41) different from; (<u>Explanation</u>: Empirical data indicate that there are likely to be some variation in the sample statistics compared with the population from which the samples are selected which have fixed values.)

(2.42) sample means; (<u>Explanation</u>: The standard error of the mean is the standard deviation of the distribution of the means of equal-size samples that are selected from a given population.)

(2.43) confidence interval; (<u>Explanation</u>: Confidence intervals is used to estimate the range of the population values. Effect size is used to evaluate the practical significance of the results, not to predict the population values.)

(2.44) d;

(2.45) a;

(2.46) d;

(2.47) b;

(2.48) c;

(2.49) b;

Chapter 3

ORGANIZING AND GRAPHING DATA

Circle the <u>correct</u> answer:

3.1.   Class intervals are usually created when the range of the scores is **<u>high/low</u>**.

3.2.   Tables that are used to indicate the number of scores at or above a given score are called **<u>class intervals/cumulative frequencies</u>** tables.

3. 3.   A graph where each bar represent a category, and the bars are typically ordered by their height, is called a **<u>bar diagram/histogram</u>**.

3.4.   The two graphs that are used to depict frequency distributions are the frequency polygon and the **<u>bar diagram/histogram</u>**.

3.5.   In drawing histograms, the lower scores are recorded on the **<u>left/right</u>** side of the scores axis (the horizontal axis).

3.6.   Frequency polygons are likely to look smoother as the number of scores **<u>increases/decreases</u>**.

3.7.   The graph most likely to be used to show data found in a cumulative frequencies table is the **<u>frequency polygon/ogive</u>**.

3.8.   The type of graph that can best show how different subgroups in a distribution relate to each other and how the proportions of the different subgroups add up to 100% is the **<u>bar diagram/pie graph</u>**.

3.9.   The median, skewness, and spread of a distribution are best depicted using a **<u>box plot/line graph</u>**.

Choose the most appropriate graphs for the sets of data in the following questions and explain your choices:

3.10.   Following is a list of 5 books that were read the most by the fourth-grade students at Washington school. The number of girls is the same as the number of boys in the fourth grade. The list shows the *percentages* of girls and boys who read each of the 5 books. Choose the most appropriate graph to present these data and determine whether there are gender differences in book choices. Explain your choice of a graph.

Book Title	**Girls**	**Boys**
Book A	75%	63%
Book B	69%	65%
Book C	62%	71%
Book D	65%	61%
Book E	57%	63%

3.11.   Records over the last 100 years indicate that the average temperature for the month of August is 83^0. Following is a list of the temperatures for the last 10 days of August 2004. Choose the most appropriate graph to depict this information and explain your choice. The graph that you draw should depict the fluctuations in daily temperatures around the average temperature of 83^0.

Date	**Temperature/Degrees**
August 22	81
August 23	79
August 24	76
August 25	78
August 26	77
August 27	83
August 28	85
August 29	86
August 30	91
August 31	88

3.12.   Following are two distributions of race/ethnic groups in the district for the years 1994 and 2004, reported in *percentages*. The number of students in the district remained approximately the same over these 10 years. Graph the data in the table, using the most appropriate graph. The graph that you choose should allow you to look at the racial/ethnic distribution in 1994 and in 2004 and to determine if there are changes in the two distributions. Explain your choice and interpret the graph.

Group	1994	2004
Asians	10%	12%
African Americans	25%	31%
Hispanics	10%	15%
Caucasians	42%	30%
Others	13%	12%
Total	100%	100%

3.13.   Following are the mean test scores of three 8th-grade classes (8a, 8b, and 8c) over the years 2001 to 2004. Draw the most appropriate graph to represent these statistics and explain your choice.

Class	2001	2002	2003	2004
8a	58	69	60	74
8b	70	73	75	78
8c	62	63	63	62

3.14. A group of teachers at a large high school surveyed their students to determine their opinions about being assessed using portfolios. The table below shows the students' responses, reported in percentages, by grade level. Choose the most appropriate graph to display the data and explain your choice.

Grade Level	% Preferring Portfolio Assessment
Freshmen	28
Sophomores	47
Juniors	34
Seniors	23

Answers - Chapter 3:

(3.1) high;

(3.2) cumulative frequencies;

(3.3) bar diagram;

(3.4) histogram;

(3.5) left;

(3.6) increases;

(3.7) ogive;

(3.8) pie graph;

(3.9) box plot ;

(3.10) Your choice should be a bar graph with 5 sets of joint bars. For each of the 5 books, draw two joint bars; one bar for girls and one bar for boys. The graph indicates that Books A, B, and D were preferred by more girls than boys, whereas Books C and E were preferred by more boys than girls.

(3.11) Your choice should be a line graph. The temperatures should be marked on the vertical axis and the dates should be marked on the horizontal axis. To show the average temperature of 83^0 for the month, draw a line parallel to the horizontal axis, starting at the 83^0 point. The graph shows that for the first 5 days in August the temperatures were below normal and for the last 4 days the temperatures were above normal.

(3.12) You should draw two pie graphs representing the racial/ethnic group distributions in the district in 1994 and 2004. Each wedge in the pies represents a racial/ethnic group in the district. An inspection of the two pies shows some changes in the racial/ethnic make-up of the district from 1994 to 2004. The percentage of Caucasian students *decreased* while the percentages of African American and Hispanic students increased. The percentages of Asians and Others remained about the same.

(3.13) Use a line graph to show trends and changes over time and compare the three classes. The vertical axis in the graph should show the test scores and the horizontal axis should show the years (2001 to 2004). The graph should have 3 horizontal lines representing the three 8th-grade classes. The graph indicates that 8b scored the highest in all 4 years and is on an upward trend; 8c scored the lowest and its scores were very similar over the 4 years; 8a had inconsistent scores, which were low in the first and third year and high in the second and fourth year.

(3.14) Draw a bar graph where each bar represents the responses of one grade level. The vertical axis should be used to record the percentages of students who prefer portfolio assessment and the horizontal axis should show the four grade levels. The graph shows that there is no clear relationship between students' grade level and their preferences. Sophomores and juniors prefer portfolios assessment more than do freshmen and seniors. The bars can be drawn vertically or horizontally.

<u>Note</u>: If the bars were ordered by grade level, the bars would not be ordered by height. If the bars were ordered by height, the grade levels would not be properly ordered.

Chapter 3

Supplemental Microsoft® Excel Exercises[2]

S3.1.   Open the "DRA.xls" datafile.

S3.2   Click on the "Summary" tab to see mean pretest and posttest scores for all teachers. Generate a bar graph displaying mean pretest and posttest scores for teachers at Reed Elementary. (Specify data in "Rows" to create Pretest and Posttest scores for the X axis).

a) Do students score higher on the pretest or posttest?

b) Are the results the same across all classrooms?

> **Tech Tips:**
> To create a bar graph with vertical bars for both pretest and posttest, highlight the data in the spreadsheet and click on the graph icon on the toolbar. Select "column" as the graph type (data are in rows)
>
> Use the Data Analysis option under the Tools menu to calculate descriptive statistics, including measures of central tendency and variability. Check the "Summary Statistics" option in the descriptive statistics dialog box.

S3.3   Generate a scatterplot displaying the relationship between Pretest and Posttest scores for all Reed elementary data.

a) Describe how the scores are spread out on the graph. Are there any clusters of dots?

b) Find the students who received a Pretest DRA score of 15. What were their Posttest scores?

c) Describe the spread of the dots for Pretest scores below 20 versus Pretest scores above 20.

d) Is there more variability for low Pretest scores or for high Pretest scores?

---

[2]NOTE: Access the datasets and exercises online at
www.evalsolutions.com/Practical_Statistics/ index.htm

Chapter 3

Answers for Microsoft® Excel Exercises

(S3.2)

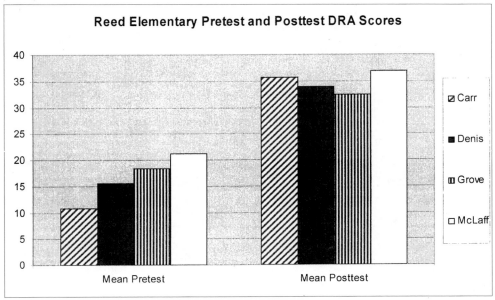

a) Students' scores are higher for the posttest.

b) The trend is similar across all teachers. All students' posttest scores are higher than their pretest scores. But Carr's classroom gained the most from pretest to posttest. Another way to depict the pre-to-post changes is to generate a pair of bar graphs for each teacher (pre and posttest for each). Simply select "columns" for your data series rather than "rows."

(S3.3)

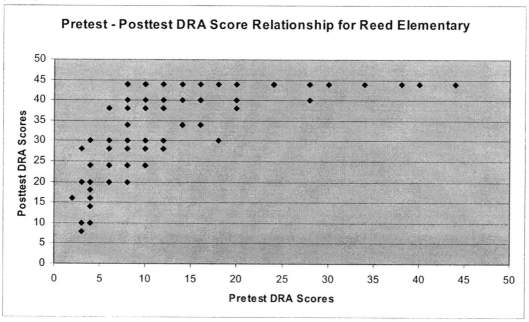

a) There are clusters of dots starting on the bottom left and continuing to about the middle of the graph (up to Pretest score=20) with a single row of dots on the right half of the graph.

b) Posttest scores = 34, 40, 44.

c) The Pretest scores below 20 are more spread out than the Pretest scores above 20.

d) There is a bigger range of scores on the Posttest for students scoring low on the Pretest.

Chapter 4

MEASURES OF CENTRAL TENDENCY

Fill in the blanks:

4.1.   The score that repeats the most often in a distribution is called the _____.

4.2.   The descriptive statistic used the most in inferential statistics as a measure of central tendency is the _____.

4.3.   The measure of central tendency used with nominal scale data is the _____

4.4.   To find the mean of a sample ($\bar{X}$), the ΣX (the sum of the scores) is divided by _____.

Circle the correct answer:

4.5.   In a *positively* skewed distribution, the majority of the scores cluster **above/below** the _____.

4.6.   The mode and the mean have the same values in distributions that are **normal/negatively skewed**.

4.7.   Distributions with few scores are **more/less** likely to have a mode than distributions with many scores.

Answer the following questions:

4.8.   Which measure of central tendency would be the most appropriate for summarizing the following test scores? Explain your choice.

13, 14, 10, 38, 11, 12, 16, 15

4.9.   What is the difference between $\bar{X}$ and μ? How are they related to each other?

4.10.   A distribution of 10 scores has a mean of <u>6</u>. Following are 9 scores of this distribution. Which score is missing (remember that the mean should be 6)?

4, 8, 10, 5, 9, 3, 6, 7, 3

4.11.   When the sum of a group of scores is 280 and the mean of the scores is 7, how many scores are in the distribution?

4.12.   Find the mode, median, and mean of the distribution depicted in the following histogram:

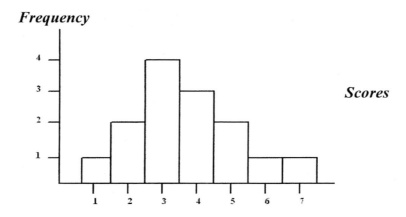

Answers - Chapter 4:

(4.1)   mode;

(4.2)   mean;

(4.3)   mode;

(4.4)   the number of the scores;

(4.5)   below;

(4.6)   normal;

(4.7)   less;

(4.8)   median. (<u>Explanation</u>: There is no mode and the mean is 16.13, which is higher than 7 out of 8 scores in the distribution.)

(4.9) $\bar{X}$ is the mean of a sample and μ is the mean of a population. In inferential statistics, we usually obtain $\bar{X}$ and use it to estimate μ;

(4.10)   5; (<u>Explanation</u>: The sum of the scores should be 60 if there are 10 scores and the mean is 6. Adding up the 9 scores listed in the distribution gives us 55; therefore, the missing 10th score is 5.)

(4.11)   40 (<u>Explanation</u>: To find the number of scores, divide the sum of 280 by the mean of the scores which is 7);

(4.12)   mode=3, median=3.5, and mean=3.71; (<u>Explanation</u>: Following is a list of the scores and their frequency. This list would be helpful in computing the mode, median, and mean of the distribution. As can be seen, the mode is 3 [it repeats 4 times] and the median is 3.5 [7 scores are above it and 7 scores are below it]. There are 14 scores in the distribution and the sum of the scores is 52, giving us a mean of 3.71.)

Score	Freq.
1	1
2	2
3	4
4	3
5	2
6	1
7	1

Chapter 4

Supplemental Microsoft® Excel Exercises

S4.1.   Open the "DRA.xls" datafile.

S4.2.   Compute median scores for all Pretest and Posttest DRA scores for Moore Elementary. Repeat for Reed Elementary. Create a 2X2 table in Excel with the school names in the rows and "Pretest Median" and "Posttest Median" for the columns. Complete the table using data from your descriptive analyses.

> **Tech Tips:**
> To create a line graph with lines for both pretest and posttest, highlight the data in the spreadsheet and click on the graph icon on the toolbar. Select the line type with markers displayed at each data point.
>
> Use the Data Analysis option under the Tools menu to calculate descriptive statistics, including measures of central tendency and variability.
>
> Check the "Summary Statistics" option in the descriptive statistics dialog box.

S4.3.   Generate a line graph displaying the median pretest and posttest scores for Moore and Reed.

   a)   Compare the schools at the pretest.

   b)   Compare the schools at the posttest.

   c)   Describe the change for both schools from pretest to posttest.

   d)   Calculate the mean, median, and mode for all Posttest scores at Moore Elementary. Which measure is the best estimate for these DRA data (considering whether DRA scores are nominal, ordinal, interval, or ratio)? How do outliers in the data affect the different measures?

Chapter 4

Answers for Microsoft® Excel Exercises

(S4.2) Median Pretest/Posttest Scores for Moore and Reed

	Pretest Median	Posttest Median
Moore	**16**	**38**
Reed	**12**	**38**

(S4.3)

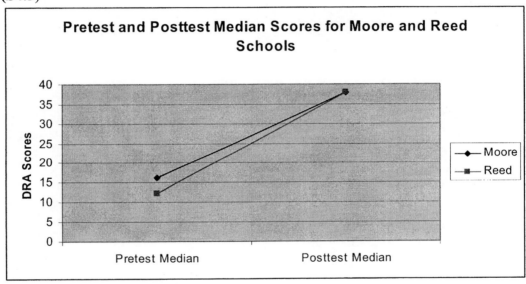

a) The schools are very similar at pretest, with Moore students scoring slightly higher.
b) The schools are the same at the posttest.
c) There is a dramatic increase in the median for the scores from the pretest to the posttest for both schools.
d) Posttest Mean=33.87, Median=38, Mode=40. The median and mode are slightly higher than the mean. Because DRA scores are ranks (ordinal data), the median score is the best estimate of central tendency. Outliers have the greatest impact on the mean.

Chapter 5

MEASURES OF VARIABILITY

Circle the <u>correct</u> answer:

5.1.   The distance between the highest and the lowest scores is called the **range/variance**.

5.2.   The SD is equal to the square root of the **mean/variance**.

5.3.   A test with 30 items is likely to have a **higher/lower** standard deviation that a test with 80 items.

5.4.   The mean of the squared deviation scores is called the **variance/standard deviation**.

5.5.   The SD of students in a gifted class taking a mathematics test is likely to be **<u>higher/lower</u>** than the SD of students in a multi-age class taking the same test.

5.6.   The SD **<u>is/is not</u>** sensitive to extreme scores.

5.7.   The variance of the *population* is represented by **<u>S^2/σ^2</u>**.

5.8.   In most cases, the variance is **<u>larger/smaller</u>** than the SD.

5.9.   The measure of variability that takes into consideration every score in the distribution is the **range/standard deviation**.

Answer/compute the following questions:

5.10.   Study the following three distributions. What are the similarities and differences between the three distributions in terms of their means, ranges, and standard deviations? (Note: Assume the three distributions to be samples if you decide to compute their standard deviations.)

Distribution A: 8, 9, 6, 12, 5
Distribution B: 7, 10, 11, 8, 4
Distribution C: 7, 9, 8, 9, 7

5.11. Three 4th-grade classes (4a, 4b, and 4c), each with 26 students, took the same language arts test. The SD of 4a was 7; the SD of 4b was 16; and the SD of 4c was 10. Which class was more *homogeneous* in regard to the scores on the language arts test?

5.12. Means and standard deviations were calculated for a Total Reading test with 45 items. This test is comprised of 20 Reading Comprehension and 25 Vocabulary items. Estimate which of the following standard deviations was obtained for the Total Reading test and which standard deviation was obtained for the Vocabulary test.

a. SD = 5.7   b. SD = 8.3

5.13. Eight judges were selected to judge the statewide gymnastic competition. As part of their training, all judges observed a videotape of one gymnast in competition, and were asked to assign the gymnast a rating on a scale of 1-10. After 1 week of training and workshops, the eight judges were asked again to watch the same videotape, and rate the gymnast's performance, using the same scale of 1-10.

Review the following scores. Is there a difference between the pretraining and posttraining rating scores? What effect, if any, did the training have on the judges? Explain.

Judge	Pretraining	Posttraining
A	9.5	9.1
B	7.8	8.9
C	9.9	9.1
D	8.6	8.8
E	8.2	8.8
F	9.6	9.0
G	8.6	8.9
H	9.1	9.0
Mean	8.91	8.95
SD	0.73	0.12

5.14.   Following is a graph showing two distributions of scores of two seventh-grade classes who had taken the same test. The means and standard deviations of the two groups are also given. Estimate which of the two means and which of the two SDs belong to each group of students.

Mean = 53   SD = 7
Mean = 69   SD = 15

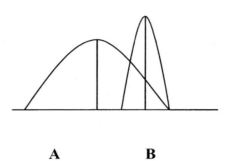

A   **B**

Group A: The mean is _____ and the SD is _____
Group B: The mean is _____ and the SD is _____

Answers - Chapter 5:

(5.1) range;

(5.2) variance;

(5.3) lower;

(5.4) variance;

(5.5) lower; (<u>Explanation</u>: There are likely to be fewer differences and less variability in the scores of students in a gifted class compared with a multi-age class.)

(5.6) is;

(5.7) σ^2;

(5.8) larger; (<u>Explanation</u>: The SD is the square root of the variance.)

(5.9) standard deviation; (<u>Explanation</u>: The range is determined by the highest and lowest scores in the distribution only and it is not affected by other scores.)

(5.10) The means of all three distributions are 8; the ranges and standard deviations of Distributions A and B are the same (range=7; SD=2.74); the range of Distribution C is the smallest (range=3) and its SD is the lowest (SD=1.00);

(5.11) 4a; (<u>Explanation</u>: The SD of 4a is the lowest)

(5.12) The SD of the Total Reading test is 8.3 and the SD of the Vocabulary test is 5.7; (<u>Explanation</u>: The Total Reading test, with 45 items, is longer than the Vocabulary test, with 25 items; therefore, it is expected to have a higher SD);

(5.13) The means of pretraining and posttraining scores are about the same, but the SD of the posttraining scores is much smaller. It seems that, as a result of the training, the 8 judges are better informed and more consistent in the scores they assign (a lower SD on the posttraining scores).

(5.14) Group A: mean=53, SD=15; Group B: mean=69, SD=7; (<u>Explanation</u>: The mean of Group B is higher than the mean of Group A, and the SD of Group A is higher than the SD of Group B [a wider spread of scores in Group A].)

Chapter 5

Supplemental Microsoft® Excel Exercises

S5.1   Open the "ITBS.xls" datafile.

S5.2   Calculate the standard deviation, variance, and range for the five variables (Grade, Reading S.S, Language S.S, and Math S.S.).

S5.3   Review the analysis results to answer these questions.

   a) Compare the standard deviation for the three measures.

> **Tech Tips:**
> Use the Data Analysis option under the Tools menu to calculate descriptive statistics, including measures of central tendency and variability.
>
> Check the "Summary Statistics" option in the descriptive statistics dialog box.

   b) Compare the variance for the three measures.

   c) Compare the range for the three measures.

S5.4. Review the analysis results to answer these questions.
   a) Which variable (reading, language, and math) shows the **highest variations** (or differences) in responses by the students? How can you tell?

   b) Which variable (reading, language, and math) shows the **most similar** responses by the students?

c) What do these trends mean about students' achievement on these subtests?

S5.5. Evaluate the statistics you calculated for the above variables. Do any of them seem inappropriate? Explain.

Chapter 5

Answers for Microsoft® Excel Exercises

(S5.2)

GEND.		GRADE		READ (S.S.)		MATH (S.S.)		LANG (S.S.)	
Mean	1.56	Mean	0.98	Mean	153.82	Mean	150.12	Mean	150.84
Std. Err	0.03	Std. Err	0.05	Std. Err	1.43	Std. Err	0.98	Std. Err	1.08
Median	2	Median	1	Median	153	Median	150	Median	152
Mode	2	Mode	0	Mode	132	Mode	138	Mode	140
Stand. Dev.	0.5	Stand. Dev.	0.82	Stand. Dev.	24.99	Stand. Dev.	17.08	Stand. Dev.	18.79
Sample Var.	0.25	Sample Var.	0.68	Sample Var.	624.26	Sample Var.	291.87	Sample Var.	353.12
Kurt	-1.9	Kurt	-1.53	Kurt	1.85	Kurt	-0.52	Kurt	-0.61
Skew	-0.3	Skew	0.04	Skew	0.72	Skew	0.33	Skew	0.21
Range	1	Range	2	Range	165	Range	86	Range	99
Min	1	Min	0	Min	100	Min	110	Min	112
Max	2	Max	2	Max	265	Max	196	Max	211
Sum	480	Sum	301	Sum	46915	Sum	46089	Sum	45856
Count	307	Count	307	Count	305	Count	307	Count	304

*Note: Decimals rounded

a) The standard deviations of math (σ=17.08) and language (σ =18.79) scores are similar. The standard deviation is slightly larger for reading (σ =24.99). The standard deviation is less than 1.00 for gender and grade.

b) The variances of math (σ^2=291.87) and language (σ^2=353.12) scores are similar. The variance is slightly larger for reading (σ^2=624.26). The variance is less than 1.00 for gender and grade (σ^2= 0.25; notice the variance is the square of the standard deviation).

c) The ranges of math and language scores are very similar. The range is larger for reading. The ranges for gender and grade are about the same. The values for the ranges are smaller than the variance but larger than the standard deviation for reading, math, and language scores.

(S5.4)

a) The reading scores show the most variation or differences in students. All three measures of student differences (standard deviation, variance, and range) are largest for reading.

b) The math scores show the similarity between students. All three measures of student differences (standard deviation, variance, and range) are smallest for math.

c) Students are more similar in their math achievement than they are in their reading achievement. The achievement differences in math are somewhat smaller than the achievement differences in reading for these students.

(S5.5)
Gender is a nominal variable. The scores are meaningless because the values hold no numerical information.

Chapter 6

THE NORMAL CURVE

AND STANDARD SCORES

Circle the <u>best</u> answer:

6.1.   In a normal distribution _____

        a.   the mean and SD have the same value.
        b.   the SD is always higher than the mean.
        c.   the mean and median have the same value.
        d.   the median and SD have the same value.

6.2.   In a normal curve, the percentage of scores between a z score of 0 and a z score of +1 _____

        a.   is the same as the percentage of scores between z scores of 1 and 2.
        b.   is the same as the percentage between z scores of 0 and -1.
        c.   changes as the mean changes.
        d.   cannot be estimated without further information.

6.3.   A z score of -1 converts to a T score of _____.

        a.   -1
        b.   40
        c.   60
        d.   100

6.4.   When a distribution of scores forms a normal curve _____,

        a.   the percentage of scores above the mean equals the percentage of scores below the mean.
        b.   the percentage of scores below the mean is usually higher than the percentage of scores above the mean.
        c.   the percentage of scores above the mean is usually lower than the percentage of scores below the mean.
        d.   the percentage of scores above or below the mean cannot be estimated.

6.5.   A negatively skewed distribution indicates that the scores are _____

     a.   mostly negative.
     b.   mostly low and below the mean.
     c.   distributed evenly above and below the mean.
     d.   mostly high and above the mean.

6.6.   In a normal distribution, a mean of 63 corresponds to a _____

     a.   all the answers that follow.
     b.   mode of 63.
     c.   median of 63.
     d. z score of 0.
     e. T score of 50.

6.7.   When a student has a z score of 0 it means that the student

     a.   scored above most classmates.
     b.   scored below most classmates.
     c.   scored at the mean.
     d.   failed the test.

6.8.   In a <u>positively</u> skewed distribution, which of the two is likely to be the mean and which the median?

     a. 23.50   b. 29.00

6.9.   In a <u>negatively</u> skewed distribution, which of the two is likely to be the mean and which the median?

     a. 52.00   b. 60.00

6.10.   When a student has a percentile rank of 45 it means that the student _____

     a.   answered correctly 45% of the test questions.
     b.   performed better than 45% of the examinees.
     c.   answered correctly 45 questions on the test.

6.11.   A T score of 70 is equivalent to a percentile rank of _____.

     a.   50
     b.   70
     c.   84
     d.   98

Circle the <u>correct</u> answer:

6.12. If a student receives a z score of -1, it means that the student scored **<u>above/below</u>** the mean.

6.13. As the number of scores *decreases*, the shape of the distribution is likely to become **<u>smoother/less smooth</u>**.

6.14. The percentage of scores that lies between ±1SD is **<u>68/95</u>**.

6.15. A person with a z score of +1 scored better than **<u>48%/84%</u>** of the examinees.

6.16. A *negative z* score converts to a *T* score that is **above/below** 50.

Answer/compute the following question:

6.17. Following are 3 sets of measures of central tendency (mode, median, and mean). Estimate which set represents a normal distribution, a negatively skewed distribution, and a positively skewed distribution. Explain your answer.

	<u>Mode</u>	<u>Median</u>	<u>Mean</u>
Set A	25	22	16
Set B	25	27	31
Set C	25	25	25

Set A: _____ distribution.
Set B: _____ distribution.
Set C: _____ distribution.

6.18. Following are test scores obtained by Linda on four tests (Test A, Test B, Test C, and Test D), as well as the means and standard deviations on the same four tests.

TEST	LINDA'S SCORE	MEAN	SD
Test A	54	50	8
Test B	30	27	3
Test C	69	66	6
Test D	61	62	5

Compare Linda's scores on the four tests and answer the following:

a. On which test did Linda do the best?
b. On which test did Linda perform the lowest?
c. On which two tests did Linda do equally well?

(Note: To answer these questions, you may want to start by converting Linda's scores on the four tests to z scores.)

6.19. A social studies test has a mean of 18 and a SD of 5. Assuming that the scores are distributed normally and using the normal curve picture below, answer the following questions:

a. Mark had a score of 23 on the test. What is his percentile rank?
b. We can estimate that 68% of the examinees that took the test scored between the score of ____ and the score of ____.
c. The top 2% of the students scored above the score of ____.

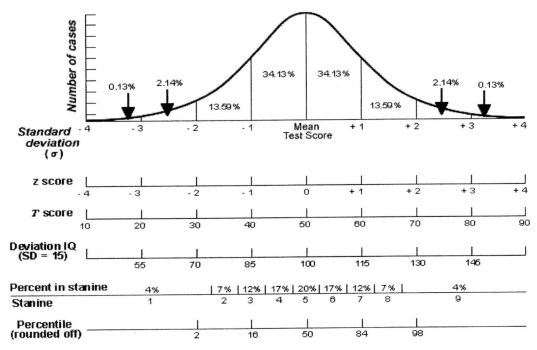

Answers - Chapter 6:

(6.1) c;

(6.2) b;

(6.3) b;

(6.4) a;

(6.5) d;

(6.6) a;

(6.7) c;

(6.8) The mean is 29.00 and the median is 23.50; <u>Explanation</u>: In a positively skewed distribution, the mean is higher than the median, because extreme high scores [i.e., outliers] pull the mean toward them.)

(6.9) The mean is 52.00 and the median is 60.00; <u>Explanation</u>: In a negatively skewed distribution, the median is higher than the mean, because extreme low scores [i.e., outliers] pull the mean toward them.)

(6.10) b;

(6.11) d; (<u>Explanation</u>: An inspection of the normal curve indicates that a T score of 70 corresponds to a z score of +2 and to a percentile rank of 98.)

(6.12) below;

(6.13) less smooth;

(6.14) 68%;

(6.15) 84%;

(6.16) below;

(6.17) Set A is a negatively skewed distribution; (<u>Explanation</u>: In Set A, the mean is lower than the median, and the median is lower than the mode, which is typical of negatively skewed distributions.) Set B is a positively skewed distribution; (<u>Explanation</u>: In Set B, the mean is higher than the median, and the median is higher than the mode, which is typical of positively skewed distributions.) Set C is a normal distribution. (<u>Explanation</u>: In Set C, the mode, median, and mean have the same value, which is typical of normal distributions.)

(6.18) a. Test B; (<u>Explanation</u>: Linda's z score is 1.00.)

       b. Test D; (<u>Explanation</u>: Linda's z score is –0.20.)

       c. Test A and C; (<u>Explanation</u>: On both tests, Linda's z scores are 0.50.)

(6.19) a. 84; (<u>Explanation</u>: Mark scored 1SD above the mean and did better than 84% of the examinees.)

       b. between the score of 13 and the score of 23; (<u>Explanation</u>: These scores are equal to ±1SD.)

       c. 28; (<u>Explanation</u>: The top 2% of the students are found in the area that is above 2SD. The point of 2SD corresponds to a score of 28.)

<u>Note</u>: Using the picture of the normal curve, you may want to mark the center with the mean of 18. Because the SD is 5, move up and down the tick marks on the horizontal axis of the normal curve by increments of 5 points in each direction. Therefore, 1SD would correspond to a score of 23 (18+5) and 2SD would correspond to a score of 28. On the other side that is below the mean, -1SD would correspond to a score of 13 (18-5) whereas −2SD would correspond to a score of 8.

Chapter 7

INTERPRETING TEST SCORES

Circle the best answer:

7.1.   A national norming group that is used by test publishers is usually comprised of examinees from a _____.

      a.   stratified random sample
      b.   random sample
      c.   sample of convenience
      d.   systematic sample

7.2.   A percentile of 50 corresponds to a stanine of _____.

      a.   2
      b.   5
      c.   6
      d.   9

7.3.   Stanine 6 includes the same number of examinees as stanine _____

      a.   1
      b.   3
      c.   4
      d.   8

7.4.   In a norm-referenced test, the highest number of examinees are expected to score in stanine ____.

      a.   1
      b.   3
      c.   5
      d.   7

Fill in the blanks:

7.5.   Manuals of commercial norm-referenced tests should include information about the demographic characteristics of the _____ that was used to generate the test norms.

7.6. In criterion-referenced tests, the performance of an individual student is compared to _____.

7.7. Prospective school psychologists are notified that they have to score at least 1SD above the mean in order to pass the state certification examination. The certification examination has mean of 50 and a SD of 12. In order to pass the examination, applicants should obtain a score of *at least* ____.

7.8. Using the same information provided in the previous question (about the state certification examination with a mean of 50 and a SD of 12), we can say that an applicant with a score of 74 performed better than _____ % of the examinees that took the certification examination.

7.9. Assuming a normal distribution, a student who obtains a *z* score of +1 on a test with a mean of 65 and a SD of 10 has a percentile rank of ___.

7.10. Students in a K-5 school district take a group IQ test. The teachers in that school district are told that they should refer to special services all students who score 1SD below the mean, or less, on the IQ test. The test has a mean of 100 and a SD of 15. Knowing this information, we can conclude that the IQ scores of students that are referred to special services are not higher than ___ .

7.11. In a school where students are tested at the same time each year, an average-level student who obtained a GE of 6.2 while in *sixth* grade is expected to get a GE of _____ when tested in the *seventh* grade.

Circle the <u>correct</u> answer:

7.12. Items that are written specifically to *maximize* the differences among examinees are found usually in **criterion-reference/norm-referenced** tests.

7.13. Overall, items in a criterion-referenced test are **easier/more difficult** than those in a norm-referenced test.

7.14. The percentile rank of a student who scored 1SD below the mean on a norm-reference achievement test is **16/34**.

7.15. Easy items on a norm-referenced test are usually placed at the **end/beginning** of the test.

7.16. The *local* norms of students in a school district known for its high academic achievement scores are expected to be **higher/lower** than the *national* percentiles obtained by these students on the same test.

Answers - Chapter 7:

(7.1) a;

(7.2) b;

(7.3) c;

(7.4) c;

(7.5) norming group;

(7.6) certain criteria;

(7.7) 62; (<u>Explanation</u>: In a test with a mean of 50 and a SD of 12, a score of 62 is 1SD above the mean [50+12=62]);

(7.8) 98; (<u>Explanation</u>: A score of 74 is 2SD above the mean, which means the applicant scored better than 98% of the examinees.)

(7.9) 84; (<u>Explanation</u>: Looking at the normal curve, we can determine that a z score of +1 corresponds to a percentile rank of 84.)

(7.10) 85; (<u>Explanation</u>: An IQ score of 85 is 1SD below the mean; therefore, in order to be referred to special services, students cannot have IQ scores that are higher than 85.)

(7.11) 7.2; (<u>Explanation</u>: Average-level students are expected to move up 1 GE each year.)

(7.12) norm-referenced; (<u>Explanation</u>: Norm-referenced test designed to spread the scores and create a bell shape distribution.)

(7.13) easier; (<u>Explanation</u>: Unlike norm-referenced test, items on criterion-referenced tests are designed to be answered correctly by the majority of the students taking the test.)

(7.14) 16; (<u>Explanation</u>: Looking at the normal curve graph, we can see that students who score 1SD below the mean perform better than 16% of the examinees.)

(7.15) beginning; (<u>Explanation</u>: Placing easier items near the beginning of the test, or sections, is done to encourage and motivate the students taking the test.)

(7.16) lower; (<u>Explanation</u>: Local percentiles compare students to other high-ability students in the district, while the national percentiles compare students to the national norming sample that includes students with low ability levels.)

Chapter 8

CORRELATION

Fill in the blanks:

8.1. The magnitude of the correlation is indicated by the correlation _____ which can range from -1.00 to +1.00.

8.2. The most common and efficient way to present the correlations of several variables with each other is by using a(n) _____ table.

8.3. The correlation between two variables can be shown *graphically* by a _____.

8.4. The null hypothesis predicts that the correlation coefficient is equal to _____.

8.5. The Spearman rank order correlation is used when the variables to be correlated are measured on a(n) _____ scale.

Circle the **correct** answer:

8.6. The hypothesis that states that $r \neq 0$ is an example of a(n) **alternative/null** hypothesis.

8.7. When an *increase* in one variable is associated with a *decrease* in the other variable, the correlation between these two variables is **positive/negative**.

8.8. In order to use the Pearson product-moment correlation, the variables to be correlated should be measured on an **ordinal/interval** scale.

8.9. When the points on a scattergram go from the bottom left to the top right they represent a **positive/negative** correlation.

8.10. The true correlation between two variables may be *underestimated* when the variance of one of the variables is **very high/very low**.

8.11. When the null hypothesis is rejected at $p < .001$, it means that the chance that $r = 0$ is **very small/very high**.

8.12. The null hypothesis is rejected when the *obtained* correlation coefficient is **higher/lower** than the *critical* value.

Answer/compute the following questions:

8.13 Which correlation coefficient (*a* or *b*) shows a stronger relationship between the two variables being correlated?

a. $X_1 \& Y_1$: $r = .85$

b. $X_2 \& Y_2$: $r = -.94$

8.14. Following are two scattergrams (in Figure A and in Figure B). Four different correlation coefficients are listed under each scattergram. Choose the coefficient that best matches each scattergram.

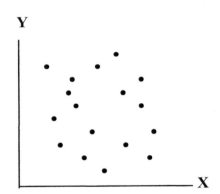

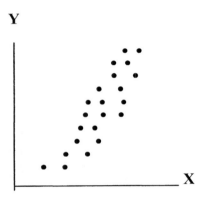

Figure A

A1. $r = .50$
A2. $r = .78$
A3. $r = -.10$
A4. $r = -.89$

Figure B

B1. $r = -.57$
B2. $r = .92$
B3. $r = .38$
B4. $r = -.91$

8.15   Following is a scattergram showing the scores of 8 students on two tests, *X* and *Y*. Each of the first 7 students is represented by a dot and their scores are listed in the table that follows. Use the scattergram to find the scores of student #8 on test *X* and test *Y*. The location of this student on the scattergram is represented by a large dot (•) next to number 8.

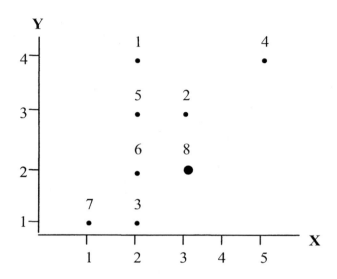

Student #	X	Y
1	2	4
2	3	3
3	2	1
4	5	4
5	2	3
6	2	2
7	1	1
8	?	?

8.16   What do these two scattergrams have in common?

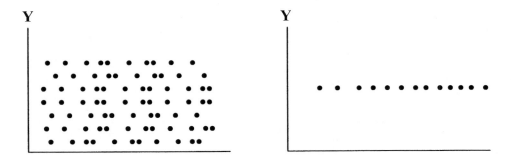

8.17   <u>Estimate</u> (***do not <u>calculate</u>!***) the correlation between Test X and Test Y that were obtained by 5 students. Indicate whether the correlation is positive or negative, and whether it is high or low. Explain your answer.

Student #	**X**	**Y**
1	21	83
2	15	70
3	17	68
4	25	90
5	19	74

8.18   <u>Estimate</u> (***do not <u>calculate</u>!***) which of the two sets of scores (A&B or X&Y) has a higher correlation. Explain your answer.

Set 1				**Set 2**		
Student#	**A**	**B**		**Student #**	**X**	**Y**
1	41	50		1	66	47
2	41	47		2	53	36
3	38	43		3	50	45
4	30	39		4	48	38
5	28	37		5	45	39

8.19   Match the correlation coefficient and the diagram illustrating this correlation.

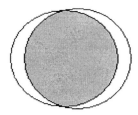

a. $r = .91$
b. $r = .28$
c. $r = .15$

8.20.   Study the following intercorrelation table. Two tests measure *language arts* and two tests measure *mathematics*. Knowing that Test 1 measures language arts, speculate which is the other language arts test (2, 3, or 4) and which two tests measure mathematics. (*A hint: the two language arts tests should correlate higher with each other than with the two mathematics tests, and the two mathematics tests should correlate higher with each other than with the two language arts tests.*)

	2	3	4
1	.35	.89	.23
2		.39	.92
3			.34

8.21.   Following are results from a study correlating science and mathematics scores from a group of 16 boys, a group of 15 girls, and the two groups combined.

Group	Correlation (*r*)/

	Group Size (*n*)/ Significance (*p* value)
BOYS	$r = .59$ $n = 16$ $p = .02$
GIRLS	$r = .52$ $n = 15$ $p = .05$
COMBINED	$r = .53$ $n = 31$ $p = .01$

a. Which correlation coefficient is the highest?
b. Which correlation coefficient has the highest statistical significance?
c. How can a correlation of $r=.53$ (from the combined group) be more statistically significant (better p value) than a correlation of $r=.59$ (from the group of boys)?

Answers - Chapter 8:

(8.1)   coefficient;

(8.2)   intercorrelation;

(8.3)   scattergram;

(8.4)   zero;

(8.5)   ordinal

(8.6)   alternative;

(8.7)   negative;

(8.8)   interval;

(8.9)   positive;

(8.10) very low;

(8.11) very small;

(8.12) higher;

(8.13) b; (<u>Explanation</u>: Even though the correlation coefficient of -.94 is negative, it represents a stronger relationship between the variable than the coefficient of .84.)

(8.14) Figure A matches the correlation of $r=$ -.10 in A3; (<u>Explanation</u>: The scattergram in Figure A shows a low negative correlation corresponding to $r=$ -.10). Figure B matches the correlation of $r=.92$ in B2; (<u>Explanation</u>: The scattergram in Figure B shows a high positive correlation corresponding to $r=.92$.)

(8.15) X=3 and Y=2; (<u>Explanation</u>: Locate the dot for student #8. Next, draw a vertical line from the dot to the X axis, and a horizontal line from the dot to the Y axis. These lines show that the score of student #8 on X is 3 and the student's score on Y is 2.)

(8.16) Both scattergrams indicate very low or no correlation;

(8.17) The correlation is positive and very high. (<u>Explanation</u>: Start by rank-ordering the scores on X and then do the same for the scores on Y. The relative positions of the 5 students on the two tests are very similar, indicating a high positive correlation. Those who scored high on one test also scored high on the other test, and those who scored low on one test also scored low on the other test.)

(8.18) The correlation between A and B is higher than the correlation between X and Y; (<u>Explanation</u>: Start by rank ordering each set of scores and comparing the ranks. You can see that the ranks of the students on Test A are similar to their ranks on Test B [in Set 1], showing a high correlation. However, the ranks of the students on Test X differ from their ranks on Test Y [in Set 2], showing a lower correlation.)

(8.19) a (r=.91); (<u>Explanation</u>: Start by squaring the three correlation coefficients to determine the *coefficients of determination*. This would reveal that diagram most closely represents the correlation coefficient of r=.91. The diagram and this coefficient both show a high level of overlap and association between the two variables.)

(8.20) Tests 1&3 measure language arts, and Tests 2&4 measure mathematics (<u>Explanation</u>: Tests 1&3 have a higher correlation with each other than with the other two tests and because Test 1 measures language arts, we can assume that Test 3 also measures language arts. Tests 2&4 have a higher correlation with each other than with the other two tests; therefore, we can assume that both tests measure mathematics.)

(8.21)   a.   The correlation of r=.59 (for the boys) is the highest.

       b.   The correlation of r=.53 (for the two groups combined), because its p value of .01 is lower than the other two p values.

       c.   The correlation of r=.53 was computed for a group of 31, while the correlation of r=.59 was computed for a group of 16.

Chapter 8

Supplemental Microsoft® Excel Exercises

S8.1.   Open the "ITBS.xls" datafile.

S8.2.   Investigate the relationship between students' reading scale scores and their math scale scores.

Write the hypothesized relationship:

a) Null Hypothesis:

_____

b) Directional Alternative Hypothesis:

_____

> **Tech Tips:**
> Use the Data Analysis option under the Tools menu to calculate the correlation.
>
> Generate the scatterplot for all data. For advanced users, use the "Series" tab to create separate clusters for Kindergarten, First, and Second graders.

S8.3.   Compute a correlation coefficient.

S8.4.   Report the variable names and correlation.

S8.5.   Is the correlation significant? (Assume the critical value = .095 with a preset significance level=.05). Explain your answer.

S8.6.   Describe the magnitude and direction of the correlation.

S8.7.   What decision can you make about the null hypothesis?

S8.8.   Create a scatterplot that shows the relationship between the math and reading scores. Are there any outliers?

Chapter 8

Answers for Microsoft® Excel Exercises

(S8.2)

    a) Null Hypothesis: The correlation of reading and math scale scores is = 0 or There is no significant correlation between reading and math scores.

    b) Alternative Directional Hypothesis: The correlation of reading and math scale scores is > 0 or There is a significant positive correlation between reading and math scores.

(S8.4)

	READING (S.S.)	MATH (S.S.)
READING (S.S.)	1	
MATH (S.S.)	0.735804	1

(S8.5) The correlation is significant for a preset significance level=.001.

(S8.6) The magnitude is .735, a strong relationship. The direction is positive. As reading scores go up, math scores go up. As reading scores go down, math scores go down. Reading scores are associated with math scores; those who score high on one variable also tend to score high on the other variable.

(S8.7) Reject the null hypothesis with a preset significance level =.05 (We only want to risk a 5% chance of committing a Type 1 Error before we compute the statistic. Our actual significance level shows even a lower actual risk of a Type 1 Error). The data supports the alternative hypothesis. There is a less than 1/10% chance of a Type 1 Error. That is, there is less than 1/10% chance that we are rejecting the null hypothesis when it really is true.

(S8.8)

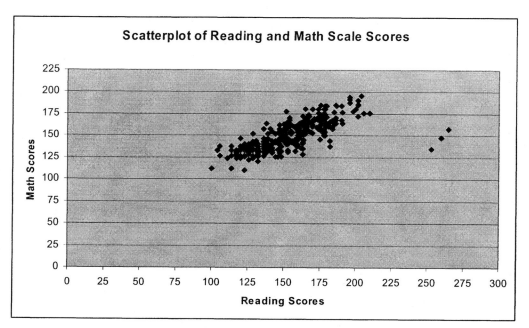

There appear to be 3 outliers for Reading scores over 250.

Chapter 9

PREDICTION AND REGRESSION

Fill in the blanks:

9.1.   In *simple* regression, there is/are _____ predictor(s).

9.2.   The regression line is also called *a line* _____ .

9.3.   The slope of the regression line is represented by the letter ____ .

9.4.   When the regression equation is used to draw a line, the point where that line intersects the vertical line (the *Y*-axis) is represented by the letter ____ which indicates the *intercept*.

9.5.   When the correlation between two variables is *perfect* and *positive*, and we use one of these variables to predict the other one, the *standard error of estimate* (S_E) is _____ .

9.6.   The difference between an actual *Y* score and its corresponding predicted *Y* score (*Y'*) is called the _____ score.

9.7.   In *multiple* regression with *two* predictors, there is/are _____ intercept(s), represented in the equation by the letter *a*.

Circle the <u>correct</u> answer:

9.8.   In regression, the *predictor* is called the **independent/dependent** variable, and the *predicted* variable (or the *criterion* variable) is called the **independent/dependent**.

9.9.   The *predicted* variable is represented by the letter **<u>X/Y</u>** and the *predictor* is represented by the letter **<u>X/Y</u>**.

9.10.   In the regression equation, the letter *b* represents the **constant/coefficient** and the letter *a* represents the **constant/coefficient**.

9.11. The dependent variable can be predicted more accurately as the correlation between the independent and dependent variables **increases/decreases**.

9.12. As the correlation between the predictor and the criterion variable *increases*, the standard error of estimate (S_E) **increases/decreases**.

9.13. The predicted Y scores are expected to be **on/around** the regression line.

9.14. The criterion is predicted more accurately when S_E is **larger/smaller**.

Answer/compute the following questions:

9.15. Study the following graph. If a student has a score of 25 on the Vocabulary Test (the predictor X), what is the student's predicted score on the Reading Test (the criterion Y)?

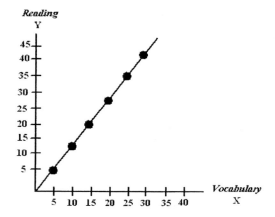

9.16. Compute S_E (the standard error of estimate) when the standard deviation of the Y-variable is 5 ($SD_Y=5$) and the correlation is 0.00 ($r=0.00$). Use the following equation to compute the S_E:

$$S_E = SD_Y\sqrt{1 - r^2} =$$

What is the relationship between the S_E (the standard error of estimate) and the SD of the dependent variable Y ($SD_Y=5$) when the correlation is zero ($r=.00$)? Explain.

9.17.   A science teacher used the midterm and final scores of her last year's students to derive a prediction equation. This year's students, who are similar to last year's students, take the midterm exam, and their scores are used to predict their final grade. The teacher decided that to get a grade of A, students have to score from 90 to 100. To get a grade of B, the scores should be 80-89, and for a grade of C, the scores should be 70-79. Following are the midterm exam scores of 6 students, and the prediction equation.

a.   Calculate the students' predicted scores (Y' scores) on the end-of-year examination. (Note: Use the prediction equation to compute the students' Y' scores.)

b.   Calculate the students' predicted final grades (a grade of A, B, or C), based on their end-of-year examination scores

Student	Students' Midterm Scores X	Predicted Final Scores Y'	Predicted Grades
Jay	52		
Dorin	45		
Sam	54		
Michael	49		
Beth	42		
Rachel	55		

$$b = 1.5 \qquad a = 13.2$$

$$Y' = b(X) + a$$

9.18.   Study the following graph, and determine what is the value of the slope of the regression line (i.e., b). Explain your answer.

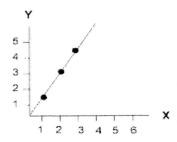

9.19.   Draw a regression line in the following graph, when the intercept is 10 (a=10), the mean of the X-variable is 20 ($\bar{X}$=20), and the mean of the Y-variable is 30 ($\bar{Y}$=30).

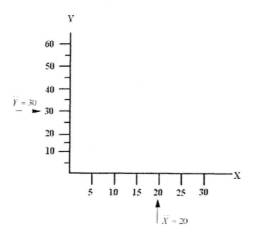

9.20.   Figure A shows three predictors, X_1, X_2, and X_3, and their correlations with the criterion variable Y_1. Figure B shows three predictors, Z_1, Z_2, and Z_3, and their correlations with a criterion variable Y_2.

    a.   Which predictor variables, those depicted in Figure A or those depicted in Figures B, correlate higher *with each other*?

    b.   Which set of three predictors, those shown in Figure A (X_1, X_2, and X_3) or those shown in Figure B (Z_1, Z_2, and Z_3) is likely to predict the criterion variables (Y_1 or Y_2) more accurately?

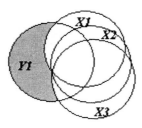

Figure A

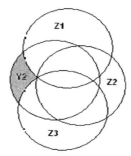

Figure B

Answers - Chapter 9:

(9.1)   one;

(9.2)   of best fit;

(9.3)   *b*;

(9.4)   *a*;

(9.5)   zero;

(9.6)   error;

(9.7)   one;

(9.8)   independent; dependent;

(9.9)   *Y, X*;

(9.10) coefficient; constant;

(9.11) increases;

(9.12) decreases;

(9.13) on;

(9.14) smaller;

(9.15) 35; (<u>Explanation</u>: Draw a straight vertical line starting at the score of 25 on the *X*-axis [Vocabulary]. When that straight line hits the regression line, make a 90-degree angle and draw a horizontal line towards the *Y*-axis. That horizontal line will intersect the *Y*-axis at a Reading score of 35.)

(9.16) The S_E is 5, the same as the SD of the dependent variable (SD_Y); (<u>Explanation</u>: When the correlation is zero [$r = .00$], the standard error of estimate [S_E] is always equal to the SD of the *Y*-variable [the criterion variable]. The calculations are as follows:

$$S_E = S_Y \sqrt{1 - r^2} = 5\sqrt{1 - .00^2} = 5\sqrt{1} = 5$$

(9.17) The predicted scores and letter grades are listed in the table below; (<u>Explanation</u>: The prediction equation was used first to compute the students' *Y'* scores. Using the information provided in the question [$b = 1.5$; $a = 13.2$], we first create the prediction equation below. To compute each student's *Y'* score, the student's *X* score is entered into the equation. The predicted scores [*Y'* scores] are then converted into letter grades. The prediction equation used for prediction is:

$$Y' = b(X) + a = 1.5(X) + 13.2$$

Student	Students' Midterm Scores X	Predicted Final Scores Y'	Predicted Grades
Jay	52	91.2	A
Dorin	45	80.7	B
Sam	54	94.2	A
Michael	49	86.7	B
Beth	42	76.2	C
Rachel	55	95.7	A

(9.18) The slope of the line (the coefficient b) is 1.5. Using the graph we can see that for every increase of 1 point on the X-variable, there is an increase of 1.5 points on the Y-variable.

(9.19) Remember that the regression line starts at the a-intercept (the starting point on the Y-axis, which is 10 in our example) and it goes through the intersection of the two means, $\bar{X}$ and $\bar{Y}$; (Explanation: In order to find the intersection of the two means, draw a straight *vertical* line, starting at $X=20$ [which is the mean of X]. Next, draw a straight *horizontal* line, starting at $Y=30$ [which is the mean of Y]. Finally, draw the regression line, starting at the intercept a [$Y=10$ in our example] and going through the point where the two means [the vertical and horizontal lines] intersect.)

(9.20) a.   The three variables depicted in Figure A correlate higher with each other than the three variables depicted in Figure B; (Explanation: The variables in Figure A depict higher correlations between the predictors X_1, X_2, and X_3, because they overlap more than those in Figure B.)

b.   The predictors shown in Figure B (Z_1, Z_2, and Z_3) are likely to predict the criterion variable Y_2 more accurately than the predictors shown in Figure A; (Explanation: The variables depicted in Figure B overlap less with each other than those in Figure A and thus account for more of the variability in the criterion variable.)

Chapter 9

Supplemental Microsoft® Excel Exercises

S9.1. Open your "ITBS_REGRESSION.xls" datafile.

S9.2. Investigate whether kindergarten and first grade reading scores are good predictors of second grade reading scores.

Compute a regression using kindergarten (X_1) and first grade scores (X_2) to predict second grade scores (Y).

Interpreting your **REGRESSION** results:

S9.3   Complete the table based on results from your Microsoft®
        Excel analyses.

Tech Tip:
To compute a REGRESSION, select "Regression" from the Data-Analysis dialog box under "Tools" menu.

Highlight the columns of your independent (predictor) variables for "X" and dependent (outcome) variables for "Y" in the dialog box. Be sure to specify a 95% or more confidence interval.

SUMMARY OUTPUT

Regression Statistics	
Multiple R	
R Square	
Adjusted R Square	
Standard Error	
Observations	

	Coefficients	Standard Error	P-value
Intercept			
Kindergarten READING (S.S.)			
First Grade READING (S.S.)			

S9.4   Identify the <u>predictor</u> and <u>dependent</u> variables in your analyses.

S9.5   Identify the R and *p* values.

S9.6   a) Identify R^2.

b) What does this indicate about the amount of variance accounted for by these independent variables?

c) Are the kindergarten and first grade scores good predictors of second grade scores?

S9.7   a) Based on your analyses, what is the value of knowing kindergarten and first grade scores in reading? How can educators use this information to predict student achievement?

b) How might keeping track of these scores over time be used as part of a school improvement plan?

Chapter 9

Answers for Microsoft® Excel Exercises

(S9.3)
SUMMARY
OUTPUT

Regression Statistics	
Multiple R	0.94979
R Square	0.902101
Adjusted R Square	0.900018
Standard Error	6.541308
Observations	97

	Coefficients	Standard Error	P-value
Intercept	2.9854	14.74103	0.839944
Kindergarten READING (S.S.)	2.2627	0.32875	6.49E-10
First Grade READING (S.S.)	-0.7654	0.35416	0.033218

(S9.4) Kindergarten and first grade scores are the <u>predictors</u> and second grade score variable is the <u>dependent</u> variable.

(S9.5) R=.95, p=.00001

(S9.6) a) R^2=.902
b) Kindergarten and first grade scores account for about 90% of the differences in second grade scores.
c) Kindergarten and first grade scores are excellent predictors of second grade scores. Very little of the variance in second grade scores is left unaccounted for or unexplained.

(S9.7) a) Knowing kindergarten and first grade scores is valuable for identifying patterns in student achievement. It is likely that students' scores will be similar in second grade.

b) A school might use kindergarten and first grade achievement scores *in conjunction with* classroom-based indicators (like report cards and portfolios) to identify student learning needs. Second grade teachers can adapt instruction based on analyses of all data.

Chapter 10

t TEST

Fill in the blanks:

10.1.   In a *t* test for a single sample, the sample's mean is compared to the population _____ .

10.2.   When we use a paired-samples *t* test to compare the pretest and posttest scores for a group of 45 people, the degrees of freedom (*df*) are _____ .

10.3.   If we conduct a *t* test for independent samples, and $n_1 = 32$ and $n_2 = 35$, the degrees of freedom (*df*) are ____ .

10.4.   A researcher wants to study the effect of college education on people's earning by comparing the annual salaries of a randomly-selected group of 100 college graduates to the annual salaries of 100 randomly-selected group of people whose highest level of education is high school. To compare the mean annual salaries of the two groups, the researcher should use a *t* test for _____ .

10.5.   A technology coordinator and a science teacher in a middle school want to determine the effectiveness of a program that makes extensive use of educational technology in eighth-grade science classes. They compare the science scores of the eighth graders in the school on a state-administered test to the mean score of <u>all</u> eighth-grade students in the state on the same test. The appropriate statistical test the coordinator and the teacher should use for their analysis is the *t* test for _____ .

10.6.   As part of the process to develop two parallel forms of a questionnaire, a test constructor may administer both forms to a group of students, and then use a *t* test for _____ samples to compare the mean scores on the two forms.

Circle the <u>correct</u> answer:

10.7.   A difference of 4 points between two *homogeneous* groups is likely to be **more/less** statistically significant than the same difference (of 4 points) between two *heterogeneous* groups, when all four groups are taking the same test and have approximately the same number of students.

10.8.   A difference of 3 points on a 100-item test taken by two groups is likely to be **more/less** statistically significant than a difference of 3 points on a 30-item test taken by the same two groups.

10.9.   When a *t* test for paired samples is used to compare the pretest and the posttest means, the number of pretest scores is **the same as/different than** the number of posttest scores.

10.10.   When we want to compare whether girls' scores on the SAT are different from boys' scores, we should use a *t* test for **paired samples/independent samples**.

10.11.   In studies where the alternative (research) hypothesis is *directional*, the critical values for a **one-tailed test/two-tailed test** should be used to determine the level of significance (i.e., the *p* value).

10.12.   When the alternative hypothesis is: H_A: $\mu_1 = \mu_2$, the critical values for **one-tailed test/two-tailed test** should be used to determine the level of statistical significance.

Answer/compute the following questions:

10.13.   In a study conducted to compare the test scores of experimental and control groups, a 50-item test is administered to both groups at the end of the study. The mean of the experimental group on the test is 1 point higher than the mean of the control group. The researchers conduct a *t* test for independent samples to compare the two means. The *obtained t* value is 1.89, and the *p*-value is .05. Can we conclude that the experimental treatment was *clearly effective* because the *t* value is *statistically significant*? Explain.

10.14.   Study the following formula for a *t* test for independent samples. What measures (e.g., the mean of Group 1) are needed in order to calculate the *t* value? (Respond in words, not symbols).

$$t = \frac{\overline{X}_1 - \overline{X}_2}{\sqrt{\dfrac{(n_1 - 1)S_1^2 + (n_2 - 1)S_2^2}{n_1 + n_2 - 2}\left(\dfrac{1}{n_1} + \dfrac{1}{n_2}\right)}}$$

10.15. Identify each of the following as a *null* hypothesis, a *directional* hypothesis, or a *nondirectional* hypothesis.

a. $\mu_1 \neq \mu_2$ is a _____ hypothesis
b. $\mu_1 = \mu_2$ is a _____ hypothesis
c. $\mu_1 > \mu_2$ is a _____ hypothesis
d. $\mu_1 - \mu_2 = 0$ is a _____ hypothesis

10.16. A school psychologist wants to compare the scores of a group of 35 students on two different IQ tests: one is a group IQ test and one is an individually-administered IQ test. The psychologist compares the mean scores of the students on the two tests. Which *t* test should the psychologist use to determine whether there is a significant difference between the two sets of IQ scores? Explain.

10.17. The principal of Jefferson school wishes to determine whether there are differences between teachers and parents in their attitude toward school. At the beginning of the school year, the principal asks 30 randomly selected parents and 28 teachers to complete a 40-item questionnaire designed to measure attitudes toward school. The results are displayed in the following table:

Group	*n*	Mean	SD	*t*	*p*
Parents	30	18.30	9.85		
				1.92	.03
Teachers	28	23.07	9.07		

a.   Which *t* test should the principal use to compare the responses of the parents and the teachers? Explain.
b.   What are the degrees of freedom (*df*)?
c.   What are the conclusions of the principal based on the results in the table? Explain.

10.18. Based on the results of the study described in the previous question, the principal, the PTA, and the entire school staff decide to implement several programs to get parents more actively involved with the school. The programs include a monthly newsletter that is being sent to the parents, additional after-school activities for the students, a drug prevention program, and several open houses. At the end of the school year, the principal asks the same group of parents (*n*=30) to rate the school again, using the same questionnaire as the one used at the beginning of the year. The following table displays the results obtained by the principal:

Scores	Mean	SD	t	p
Pretest	18.30	9.85		
			7.13	.0001
Posttest	22.10	8.88		

a.   Which t test should be used to analyze the data? Explain.
b.   What are the degrees of freedom (df)?
c.   Based on the results in the table, can the principal conclude that the interventions worked? Explain.

10.19. Two third-grade teachers randomly divide last year's second grade students into two groups. One group (group 3a) includes 32 students and the second one (group 3.b) includes 30 students. After dividing the students, the teachers want to confirm that the two groups are indeed similar. They hypothesize that there is no statistically significant difference between the two groups. To compare the two groups, the teachers use ratings given by the students' second-grade teachers at the end of the previous year. The rating scale ranges from 5 ("excellent student") to 1 ("having great difficulties"). Using these ratings, the teachers conduct a t test to determine whether the two groups are similar. The results are as follows:

Group	n	Mean	SD	t
3.a	32	3.66	1.31	
				2.008
3.b	30	3.00	1.26	

$t_{crit(.05,df)} = 2.000;$ $t_{crit(.02,df)} = 2.390;$ $t_{crit(.01,df)} = 2.660$

a. Which t test was used and why?
b. What were the degrees of freedom (df)?
c. What are the teachers' conclusions? Explain.

10.20. A high-school teacher teaching a senior level English Advance Placement (AP) class with 23 students wants to know whether the scores of his students on the verbal portion of the SAT are higher than the scores of other college-bound students in the school. The mean score obtained by the AP English students on the verbal portion of the SAT is 635.13 and the mean score of <u>all</u> 678 college-bound seniors in the school on the same test is 430 ($\mu=430$). A t test is used to compare the SAT Verbal scores of the AP English students to the mean score of the college-bound seniors in the school. The results of the t test are:

$\bar{X} = 635.13$ $S^2 = 71.53$

t value $= 13.75$ $p = .0001$

a. Which t test is used and why?
b. What are the degrees of freedom (*df*)?
c. What are the teacher's conclusions? Explain.

Answers - Chapter 10

(10.1)   mean;

(10.2)   df=44; (<u>Explanation</u>: The number of people in the group minus 1.)

(10.3)   65; (<u>Explanation</u>: The degrees of freedom are computed as: $df = n_1 + n_2 - 2 = 32 + 35 - 2 = 65$) [or: $(n_1\text{-}1) + (n_2\text{-}1) = 31+34=65$].)

(10.4)   independent samples; (<u>Explanation</u>: The two groups are independent of each other.)

(10.5)   a single sample; (<u>Explanation</u>: The eighth graders comprise a sample that is compared to the population of students in the state.)

(10.6)   paired; (<u>Explanation</u>: The scores on the two forms are paired because they were obtained by the same students.)

(10.7)   more; (<u>Explanation</u>: The two *heterogeneous* groups are likely to overlap more than the two *homogeneous* groups. Therefore, a difference of 4 points between the homogeneous groups is likely to be more statistically significant.)

(10.8)   less; (<u>Explanation</u>: A difference of 3 points out of 100 points is proportionally smaller than a difference of 3 points out of 30 points.)

(10.9)   the same as; (<u>Explanation</u>: Only people for whom both pretest and posttest scores are available can participate in the study.)

(10.10) independent samples; (<u>Explanation</u>: The two genders are independent of each other.)

(10.11) one-tailed test; (<u>Explanation</u>: Directional hypotheses predict the direction of the outcomes; therefore, a one-tailed test should be used.)

(10.12) two-tailed test; (<u>Explanation</u>: This alternative hypothesis is stated as a null; therefore, a two-tailed test should be used.)

(10.13) Our conclusion is that the experimental treatment is *not* clearly effective; (<u>Explanation</u>: Although the *t* value is statistically significant, a difference of 1 point on a 50-item test probably does not indicate real differences between the two groups. Based on these results alone, we should not conclude that the intervention is effective.)

(10.14) The means of the two groups, the variances of the two groups, and the number of people in both groups;

(10.15) a.   nondirectional;
   b.   null;
   c.   directional;
   d.   null;

(10.16) A *t* test for paired samples; (<u>Explanation</u>: The two IQ scores that are gathered for each student are paired; therefore, a paired-samples *t* test should be used.)

(10.17) a.   A *t* test for independent samples, because the two groups (parents and teachers) are independent of each other.
   b. $df = 56$ $(30 + 28 - 2 = 56)$.

c. The teachers' mean attitudes toward school was significantly (p=.03) more positive (a higher mean) than that of the parents, and slightly more uniform (a lower SD).

(10.18) a. The paired samples t test should be used, because the pretest and posttest scores that are gathered for the same group of people are compared.

b. df = 29 (30-1 = 29).

c. The principal can conclude that the intervention programs were effective, because the posttest mean of 22.10 was significantly higher than the pretest mean of 18.30 (p=.0001). The posttest SD was lower than the pretest SD, indicating less variability in parents' attitudes after the intervention programs. However, the mean posttest score of 22.10 on the 40-item questionnaire indicates that even though there was a statistically significance improvement in parents' attitudes, it is still not very high.

(10.19) a. A t test for independent samples, because the two classrooms are independent of each other.

b. df=60 (32+30-2=60)

c. Although the two groups are selected at random, the mean score of group 3a (which is 3.66) is higher than the mean of group 3b (which is 3.00). We can report the level of significance as "p<.05". The standard deviations of the two groups are approximately the same. Note also that the obtained t value of 2.008 is very close to the critical value of 2.000 (under p=.05).

(10.20) a. A t test for a single sample, because the mean score of the AP class (the sample) is compared to μ, the mean of the population. (The other college-bound seniors in the school are considered the population.)

b. df=22 (df = 23-1=22);

c. The difference between the mean score of the AP students and the mean score of the other college-bound students is 205.13 points (635.13-430=205.13). There is a *very* slight chance (p = .0001) that this difference could have been obtained by chance alone. The teacher can be quite confident in the conclusion that the AP English students score higher than the rest of the college-bound seniors in the school.

Chapter 10

Supplemental Microsoft® Excel Exercises

S10.1. Open the file "ISEL.xls"

S10.2. You are interested in investigating the change in students' ISEL reading scores from your fall pretest to your spring posttest.

Write the hypothesized relationship:

a) Null Hypothesis:_____

b) Alternative Hypothesis:_____

S10.3. Compute a paired-samples *t* test, comparing *ISEL pre% correct* scores to *ISEL post% correct* scores for Snapshots 1-4 (Columns FG, JK, NO, RS). Complete the following table:

Snapshot 1   Pretest mean: _____   Posttest mean: _____

Pretest SD: _____   Posttest SD: _____

n: _____

t-value: _____   *p*-value: _____

Snapshot 2   Pretest mean: _____   Posttest mean: _____

Pretest SD: _____   Posttest SD: _____

n: _____

t-value: _____   *p*-value: _____

Snapshot 3   Pretest mean: _____   Posttest mean: _____

Pretest SD: _____   Posttest SD: _____

n: _____

t-value: _____   *p*-value: _____

Snapshot 4   Pretest mean: _____   Posttest mean: _____

Pretest SD: _____   Posttest SD: _____

n: _____

t-value: _____   *p*-value: _____

S10.4. Are these one tail or two tail significance tests? Explain.

S10.5. Describe the gain from Pretest to Posttest for each of the Snapshots.

S10.6 Using data from the table you completed in S7.3, first create a new table in Excel with 4 columns (Snapshots 1 – 4) and two rows (Pretest Mean, Posttest Mean). Now create a clustered bar graph for your new table that displays the changes from pretest to posttest for the four snapshots.

Chapter 10

Answers for Microsoft® Excel Exercises

(S10.2) a) Null Hypothesis: Fall ISEL Reading scores = Spring ISEL Reading scores OR there is no significant difference between the fall and spring ISEL reading scores.

        b) AlternativeHypothesis: Fall ISEL Reading Scores < Spring ISEL Reading Scores OR Fall ISEL Reading Scores are significantly lower than Spring ISEL Reading Scores.

(S10.3)

t test: Paired Two Sample for Means								
	Pre %1	*Post %1*	*Pre %2*	*Post %2*	*Pre %3*	*Post %3*	*Pre %4*	*Post %4*
Mean	75.53	97.48	68.2698	86.86	65.4667	90.733	61.48	93.37
Var	868.10	63.79	357.12	179.94	776.71	274.37	1087.9	231.3
Obs	300	300	300	300	300	300	300	300
Pears Corr.	0.5537		0.691		0.5476		0.59	
Hyp Mean Diff	0		0		0		0	
df	299		299		299		299	
t Stat	-14.67		-23.56		-18.75		-20.5	
P(T<=t) one-tail	2.22E-37		2.05E-70		1.16E-52		3.04E-59	
t Crit 1 tail	1.64996		1.64996		1.64996		1.64996	
P(T<=t) 2 tail	4.4E-37		4.1E-70		2.3E-52		6.1E-59	
t Crit 2 tail	1.96793		1.96793		1.96793		1.96793	

*Note: Decimals have been rounded.

t test results for Snapshot 1	*t* test results for Snapshot 2	*t* test results for Snapshot 3	*t* test results for Snapshot 4

Snapshot 1	Pretest mean:	75.53	Posttest mean:	97.48
	Pretest SD:	29.46	Posttest SD:	7.99
	n:	300		
	t-value:	-14.6703	*p*-value:	.00001

Snapshot 2	Pretest mean:	68.27	Posttest mean:	86.86
	Pretest SD:	18.9	Posttest SD:	13.4
	n:	300		
	t-value:	-23.5597	*p*-value:	.00001

Snapshot 3	Pretest mean:	65.47	Posttest mean:	90.73
	Pretest SD:	27.87	Posttest SD:	16.56
	n:	300		
	t-value:	-18.739	*p*-value:	.00001

Snapshot 4	Pretest mean:	61.48	Posttest mean:	93.37
	Pretest SD:	37.99	Posttest SD:	15.21
	n:	300		
	t-value:	-20.5011	*p*-value:	.00001

All gains from pretest to posttest are statistically significant. Note the differences in standard deviations between Pretest and Posttest for each snapshot. The scores are more similar for the posttest as indicated by the smaller standard deviation.

(S10.4) They are one-tail tests because we are predicting the direction of the outcome stating that the pretest < posttest, not merely that they are unequal.

(S10.5) The pretests are significantly lower than posttests for all four snapshots. (Note that the table presents the *p*-value for Snapshot 1-4 using an "E". For Snapshot 1, the *p*-value = 2.22E-37, indicating that the decimal precedes *37* "zeros" before 2.22. It is standard to substitute this notation as p<.0001).

(S10.6)

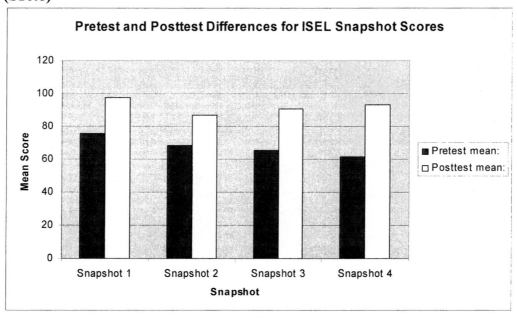

Chapter 11

ANOVA

Fill in the blanks:

11.1. While a *t* test is used to compare *two* means, the one-way ANOVA can be used to simultaneously compare _____ groups.

11.2. An ANOVA is considered to be an extension of the *t* test for independent samples because both investigate differences between _____.

11.3. By conducting a one-way ANOVA test to compare multiple (more than 2) group means <u>simultaneously</u> instead of conducting a series of *t* tests to compare these means, the potential level of _____ is reduced.

11.4. In order to apply the ANOVA test, the data should be measured on a(n) _____ or _____ scale.

11.5. The one-way ANOVA is used when there is/are _____ independent variable(s).

11.6. With 3 groups, the null hypothesis (H_o) in ANOVA is: _____.

11.7. The *total* (or *grand*) mean in ANOVA can be thought of as the mean of _____.

11.8. The SS_W (*within-groups* sum of squares) and the SS_B (*between-groups* sum of squares) are equal to the _____ sum of squares.

11.9. To find the MS_B, we divide the SS_B by _____.

11.10. To compute the *F* ratio, we divide the _____ mean square by the _____ mean square.

11.11. Factorial ANOVA is commonly used when there are at least _____ independent variables.

Circle the <u>correct</u> answer:

11.12. The following is an example of a(n) **<u>null/alternative</u>** hypothesis in ANOVA:

$\mu_1 \neq \mu_2$ and/or $\mu_1 \neq \mu_3$ and/or $\mu_2 \neq \mu_3$

11.13. Post hoc comparisons should be conducted in cases where the F ratio **<u>is/is not</u>** statistically significant.

11.14. The F ratio is likely to be statistically significant when the differences between the group means are **<u>small/large</u>**.

11.15. The F ratio is more likely to be statistically significant when it is used to analyze scores from groups that are **<u>homogeneous/heterogeneous</u>** in regard to the characteristic or behavior being measured.

Answer the following questions:

11.16. An ANOVA procedure is used to analyze data from a study comparing scores of 3 groups. Following are the obtained mean squares and the appropriate *critical values* for the F ratio at $p=.05$ and $p=.01$.

$MS_B = 26.50$ $MS_W = 3.23$

$F_{crit\,(.05,2,20)} = 3.49$ AND $F_{crit\,(.01,2,20)} = 5.85$

a.   Compute the *obtained F* ratio.
b.   Determine whether the results are statistically significant.
c.   Report your conclusions.

11.17. Three sixth-grade classes in one school (School A) took the same reading test as did 3 other sixth-grade classes in another school (School B). Following are the means and standard deviations obtained by the 3 sixth-grade classes in each of the two schools:

SCHOOL	Means 6th Grade 1	6th Grade 2	6th Grade 3	Standard Deviations 6th Grade 1	6th Grade 2	6th Grade 3
School A	50.2	52.8	53.3	2.5	3.1	2.7
School B	41.0	48.5	55.9	2.7	3.2	2.8

Two <u>separate</u> one-way ANOVA procedures are conducted to test whether the differences between the three means of the three sixth-grade classes in each of the two schools are statistically significant. *Estimate* which *F* ratio would be larger: The one resulting from analyzing the test scores obtained from the three groups in School A or the one from analyzing the test scores obtained by the three groups in School B. Explain your answer.

11.18. Three fourth-grade classes in School A took the same math test as did 3 other fourth-grade classes in School B. Following are the means and standard deviations of the 3 classes in each of the two schools:

SCHOOL	Means			Standard Deviations		
	4th Grade2	4th Grade2	4th Grade 3	4th Grade 1	4th Grade 2	4th Grade 3
School A	71.4	78.8	90.2	3.2	4.3	4.8
School B	72.1	78.6	89.3	9.3	6.6	8.7

Two <u>separate</u> one-way ANOVA procedures are used to test whether the differences between the means in each of the two schools are statistically significant. *Estimate* which *F* ratio would be larger: the one resulting from analyzing the test scores obtained by the three groups in School A or the one resulting from analyzing the test scores of the three groups in School B. Explain your answer.

11.19. Each of the two figures below (Figure A and Figure B) depicts a set of 3 distributions. Two <u>separate</u> one-way ANOVA analyses are performed to test whether there are statistically significant differences between the three means in each set and two *F* ratios are computed. Estimate which of the two *F* ratios is likely to be higher and explain your answer.

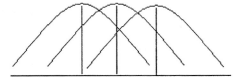

Figure A

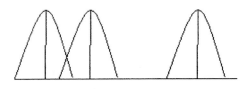

Figure B

11.20. Match the interaction shown in the following graph with one of the three *F* ratios (a, b, or c) that was calculated for the interaction. Explain your answer.

    a. $F=3.23$ $(p=.07)$

    b. $F=5.86$ $(p=.002)$

    c. $F=2.90$ $(p=.08)$

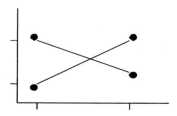

11.21. In a study comparing means of 4 groups on a reading test, the *F* ratio was significant at the $p<.05$ level. The 4 means are: Mean 1=13.12; Mean 2=9.31; Mean 3=13.65; and Mean 4=11.34. Tukey's post hoc comparison is used to test which means statistically differ from each other. The *obtained* HSD value at the $p=.05$ level is 3.74. Which means are statistically significantly different from each other? Explain.

11.22. A pilot-test study comparing two science textbooks was conducted in two schools (School A and School B). In each of the two schools, one fifth-grade class used one science textbook and the other fifth-grade class used the other science textbook. At the end of the year, all students took a standardized test in science. Following is a table listing the mean scores of the two fifth-grade classes in each of the two schools (those that used Textbook 1 and those that used Textbook 2). Study the data in the table. (*Note: Do not attempt to compute the F ratios or the exact level of significance in order to answer the questions below.*)

School	Mean of 5th Grade Students Using Textbook 1	Mean of 5th Grade Students Using Textbook 2
School A	55	53
School B	50	48

a.   Are there differences in test scores as a result of the using the two textbooks? Explain.
b.   Are there differences in performance on the science test between the two schools? Explain.
c.   Graph the interaction. Is there an interaction effect? Explain.

Answers - Chapter 11:

(11.1) two or more;

(11.2) the means of independent samples;

(11.3) error;

(11.4) interval; ratio;

(11.5) one;

(11.6) $H_o: \mu_1 = \mu_2 = \mu_3$;

(11.7) all the scores, from all the groups, combined;

(11.8) total (i.e., SS_T);

(11.9) df_B;

(11.10) *between-groups; within-groups*;

(11.11) two;

(11.12) alternative;

(11.13) is;

(11.14) large;

(11.15) homogeneous;

(11.16) a. The *F* ratio is 8.20; (Explanation: To compute the *F* ratio, divide the MS_B by the MS_W:

$$F = \frac{26.50}{3.23} = 8.20$$

b. The obtained *F* ratio of 8.20 exceeds the critical value at $p=.01$, which is 5.85. Therefore, the results are reported as statistically significant at $p<.01$.

c. We conclude that the differences between at least two of the three groups is statistically significant at $p<.01$. We reject the null hypothesis that states that there is no statistically significant difference between the means. The likelihood that our decision to reject the null hypothesis is the wrong decision is less than 1% (because the *p* value is less than .01).

(11.17) From School B, because the differences between the means of the 3 sixth-grade classes in School B are *larger* than the differences between the means of the 3 sixth-grade classes in School A. The standard deviations of the sixth-grade classes in both schools are about the same.

(11.18) From School A. Even though the means of the 3 fourth-grade classes in each of the two schools are similar to each other, the standard deviations of the 3 fourth-grade classes in School A are *smaller* than the standard deviations of the 3 fourth-grade classes in School B. Therefore, we can conclude that the 3 fourth-grade classes in school A are more distinctly different from each other, compared with 3 fourth-grade classes in School B.

(11.19) The set of distributions in Figure B. The 3 means in Figure B are farther apart from each other compared with the 3 means in Figure A (especially the mean on the right-hand side). Additionally, the 3 groups in Figure A overlap more than the 3 groups in Figure B indicating higher variability of the groups in Figure A. Therefore, an ANOVA analysis of the data depicted in Figure B is likely to result in a higher F ratio.

(11.20) b (F=5.86). The graph shows a significant interaction and the only F ratio that is statistically significant (p value of .05 or lower) is the F ratio in option b that is listed as p=.002.

(11.21) The means of groups 2&1 and the means of groups 2&3 are statistically significant because the differences between these means are higher than the HSD value of 3.74; (Explanation: To answer this question, pair all the means with each other and subtract the lower mean from the higher mean. If the difference between the means is higher than the HSD value of 3.74, that difference is considered statistically significant. Doing so, you will find that the differences between means 2&1 and 2&3 exceed the HSD value.)

(11.22) a.   Yes; the students in both schools scored higher with Textbook 1.

b.   The students in School A scored higher than the students in School B when using Textbook 1 and Textbook 2.

c.   A graph of the interaction would show that the two lines are parallel and there is no interaction effect.

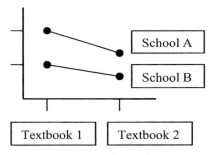

Chapter 11

Supplemental Microsoft® Excel Exercises

S11.1. Open your "ITBS_ANOVA.xls" datafile.

S11.2. Investigate whether there are differences between three groups participating in a Reading intervention: the comparison group, the group in the first year of the intervention, and the group in the second year of the intervention. Generate an ANOVA to compare the differences in the three means of the groups on the ITBS Reading scale score.

> **Tech Tip:**
> To compute a one-way ANOVA, select "ANOVA: single factor" from the Data-Analysis dialog box under "Tools" menu.
>
> Check the "columns" option in the dialog box to indicate that data are grouped in columns.

Interpreting your **ANOVA** results:

S11.3 Complete the table based on results from your Excel analyses.

Anova: Single Factor

SUMMARY

Groups	Count	Sum	Ave	Variance
Comparison Class READING (S.S.)				
1st Yr Implementation Class READING (S.S.)				
2nd Yr Implementation Class READING (S.S.)				

ANOVA

Source of Variation	SS	df	MS	F	P-value	F crit
Between Groups						
Within Groups						
Total						

S11.4 How many groups are in your analysis?

S11.5 How many students are in each group?

S11.6 Report the *F* value and *p* value. What do they indicate about the statistical significance of the test?

S11.7 Since Excel does not provide post hoc comparison tests, how might you use *t*-tests to test for significant differences?

S.11.8 Look at the means and identify the groups scoring the highest and the lowest. Though a post hoc is not available in Microsoft® Excel, how can educators look at the <u>practical difference</u> between the three means and speculate as to the effectiveness of the intervention?

Chapter 11

Answers for Microsoft® Excel Exercises

(S11.3)
Anova: Single Factor

SUMMARY

Groups	Count	Sum	Ave	Variance
Comparison Class READING (S.S.)	97	12553	129.4124	157.4532
1st Yr Imp Class READING (S.S.)	97	15064	155.299	135.6701
2nd Yr Imp Class READING (S.S.)	97	17164	176.9485	427.9661

ANOVA

Source of Variation	SS	df	MS	F	P-value	F crit
Between Groups	109884.7	2	54942.34	228.5806	3.54E-60	3.027111
Within Groups	69224.58	288	240.3631			
Total	179109.3	290				

(S11.4) There are three groups in the analysis: a comparison group, a first year group, and a second year group.

(S11.5) Comparison group n=97, First year group n=97, and Second year group n=97.

(S11.6) F=228.5806, p<.00001. The three groups are significantly different from each other. (Note that the table presents the p-value as 3.54E-60, indicating that the decimal precedes *60* "zeros" before 3.54. It is standard to substitute this notation as p<.0001).

(S11.7) You can conduct a *t*-test for each pairwise comparison (i.e., Comparison vs. First year, Comparison vs. Second year, and First year vs. Second year).

(S11.8) Looking at the scores, the Second Year reading scores for the intervention group are the highest. Educators can use their experiences with "typical" class reading averages to make judgments about whether the difference between the means of 129, 155, and 177 are <u>practically important</u>.

Chapter 12

CHI SQUARE

Fill in the blanks:

12.1. In a chi square test, the *observed* frequencies are compared to the _____ frequencies.

12.2. The null hypothesis for the chi square test states that there is no statistically significant difference between the _____ frequencies and the _____ frequencies.

12.3. In order to use a chi square test, the data have to be in the form of _____.

12.4. In order to create categories for a chi square test, observations that are measured on an interval scale should first be divided into categories in a _____ way.

12.5. The degrees of freedom (*df*) for a 3x4 chi square table are _____.

12.6. In a *goodness of fit* chi square test with 4 cells, the degrees of freedom (*df*) are _____.

Circle the <u>correct</u> answer:

12.7. A chi square test is called a *test of independence* when there is(are) **one/two** variables(s).

12.8. The chi square value increases as the differences between the *observed* and *expected* frequencies **increase/decrease**.

12.9. In a 2x2 chi square test the total number of frequencies in the first row **should always be the same as/may be different than** the total number of frequencies in the second row.

For each of the following examples, choose which type of chi square test should be used: *Goodness of fit test*, **or** *test of independence*:

12.10. To test whether a four-sided spinning top has an equal probability of landing on any of its four sides the chi square _____ should be used.

12.11. To test whether two variables are related to or are independent of each other the chi square _____ should be used.

12.12. To test whether there are differences or similarities between girls and boys in the type of books (e.g., fiction, sci-fi) they read the chi square _____ should be used.

12.13. To test whether the number of right- and left-handed students in a given school is higher than the national proportions the chi square _____ should be used.

Answer/compute the following questions:

12.14. A random sample of 100 men and 100 women were asked whether they would be willing to work as unpaid volunteers. The results indicate that 54% of the men and 64% of the women responded YES to this question, while 46% of the men and 36% of the women responded NO to the question. The chi square test was used to determine whether the men and women in the study differ in their willingness to work as unpaid volunteers. The obtained chi square value was 2.06 ($\chi^2_{(obt)}$=2.06). The appropriate critical value at p=.05 is 3.841 ($\chi^2_{crit\,(.05)}$=3.841).

    a.   Which chi square test was used to analyze the data and determine whether there are gender differences between the responses of the men and women who participated in the survey? Explain.

    b.   What was the null hypothesis for the study?

    c.   Was there a gender difference between the responses of the male and female participants? Explain.

12.15. Undergraduate students in a large state university are required to take an introduction to psychology course. Three sections of this course are offered at the same time and are taught by three different instructors. The chi square test is used to determine if any of these sections has significantly more students, which may indicate that the instructor of that section is more popular than the other two instructors. The enrollment figures for the three sections are presented in the following table. The chi square value is 6.29 (χ^2=6.29) significant at the p<.05 level.

INSTRUCTOR	NUMBER OF STUDENTS ENROLLED
Dr. Smith	114
Dr. Brown	128
Dr. Johnson	91

a. Which chi square test should be used to determine whether any of the sections has a statistically significantly higher number of students? Explain.

b. What are the *expected* frequencies?

c. What are the degrees of freedom (*df*)?

d. What are your conclusions? Explain.

12.16. Randomly selected groups of 120 parents and 150 teachers from one school district are surveyed about their attitudes toward inclusion. One of the questions asks them whether they oppose or support inclusions and their responses to this question are recorded in the following table. The data were analyzed using a chi square test. The obtained chi square value is 5.65, significant at the .02 level (*p*=.02).

GROUP	SUPPORT	OPPOSE
Parent	75	45
Teachers	72	78

a. Which chi square test should be used to analyze the data and answer the research questions? Explain.

b. Is there a statistically significant difference in the responses of the parents and teachers? Explain.

12.17. In a recent national poll, people were asked the following question: "In your opinion, how important is it to improve the nation's inner-city schools?" The responses of city residents who do not have school-age children were compared to the national responses. A chi square test was used to analyze the data in order to determine whether there is a difference in responses between those who live in cities and do not have school-age children and the national responses. The results of the study are displayed in the following table. The analysis revealed a chi square value of 4.32, significant at *p*=.36.

RESPONSE	NO CHILDREN IN SCHOOL	NATIONAL TOTALS
Very Important	78	80
Fairly Important	13	15
Not Very Important	6	3
Not Important at All	2	1
Don't Know	1	1

    a.   Which chi square test was used to analyze the data? Explain.
    b.   What was the null hypothesis?
    c.   What are the conclusions of the study? Explain.

12.18. A psychologist studying young children is interested in the development of color preferences among preschool boys. The psychologist hypothesizes that the boys would prefer certain colors to others. For the purpose of the study, only five primary colors are included: yellow, red, blue, green, and black. A group of 50 preschool boys are brought to a room and are asked to select one ball from a box full of balls. In the box there are 50 yellow balls, 50 red, 50 blue, 50 green, and 50 black. The colors of the balls chosen by the boys are recorded and a chi square test is used to analyze the data and answer the psychologist's research question. The obtained chi square value is 8.800 ($\chi^2_{obt} = 8.800$) and the appropriate critical value is $\chi^2_{crit\ (.05,4)} = 9.488$. Following are the colors chosen by the boys:

Color	No. of Times the Color Was Chosen (*Observed* Frequencies)
Yellow	6
Red	12
Blue	14
Green	4
Black	14

    a.   Which chi square test was used to analyze the data? Explain.
    b.   What are the expected frequencies?
    c.   What are the study's conclusions? Explain.

12.19. A study of 3000 girls and boys, ages 9 to 15, was conducted to explore whether there was gender and age gap in self-esteem. The study's participants were asked to respond to the statement "I'm happy with myself the way I am" by circling *Yes* or *No*. The study found that in elementary school, 60% of the girls and 67% of the boys responded *Yes*. When the same statement was posed to high school students, 29% of the girls and 48% of the boys responded *Yes*.

To answer the research questions, two chi square tests were conducted. The first one compared the responses of elementary-school girls and boys, and the second one compared the responses of high-school girls and boys. The results of the analyses are summarized in the following table. Is there a difference in the responses of girls and boys? Explain.

GROUP	PERCENT RESPONDING "YES"	χ^2	*p*
Elementary **Girls** **Boys**	60 67	0.30	.53
High School **Girls** **Boys**	29 48	4.69	.03

Answers - Chapter 12:

(12.1) expected;

(12.2) observed; expected (or: expected; observed);

(12.3) frequencies;

(12.4) logical or defensible;

(12.5) 6; (Explanation: In chi square test of independence, the *df* are computed as:[#Rows-1]x[#Columns-1]. In this example it is: [3-1]x[4-1]=6.)

(12.6) 3; (Explanation: The degrees of freedom are computed by subtracting 1 from the number of cells. In this example, the *df* are: 4-1=3.)

(12.7) two;

(12.8) increase;

(12.9) may be different than; (Explanation: Because the chi square test is used to study proportions, the total numbers of observed frequencies in the two rows do not have to be exactly the same.)

(12.10) *goodness of fit* (with equal-probability expected frequencies);

(12.11) *test of independence*;

(12.12) *test of independence*;

(12.13) *goodness of fit* (with unequal expected frequencies); (Explanation: The number of right-handed and left-handed children in the school is the *observed* frequencies and the national norms comprising the *expected* frequencies.)

(12.14) a. A 2x2 chi square *test of independence*, because there were two independent variables (gender and the response choices), each with two levels (two genders and two response choices). (Explanation: See the table below.)

Gender	Yes	No
Men	54	46
Women	64	36

b. The null hypothesis stated that there was no significant difference between the men and women in the study in their willingness to work as unpaid volunteers.

c. The obtained chi square value of 2.06 (χ^2_{obt}=2.06) does not exceed the critical value of 3.841 at the p=.05 level ($\chi^2_{crit\ (.05)}$=3.841). Therefore, we *retain* the null hypothesis. The majority of the respondents in both groups indicated that they would be willing to work as unpaid volunteers. Although more women than men were willing to volunteer, the difference between the responses of the two genders is not *statistically* significant.

(12.15) a. A *goodness of fit* chi square test with *equal* expected frequencies, because the null hypothesis is that the number of students enrolled in each of the three sections would be the same.

b. The expected frequencies are 111, 111, 111; (Explanation: Start by finding the total number of students, which is 333. To find the expected frequencies in each cell, divide the total number by 3.)

c. $df=2$; (Explanation: The degrees of freedom are the number of cells minus 1.)

d. The null hypothesis that states that there are no statistically significant differences in the numbers of students enrolled in each section is rejected at the $p<.05$ in favor of the alternative hypothesis that states that there is a significant difference in the number of students enrolled in the three sections. Specifically, Dr. Brown is the most popular instructor and Dr. Johnson is the least popular instructor.

(12.16) a. The chi square *test of independence* should be used because there are two independent variables (groups and responses).

b. We can conclude that the difference between the parents and the teachers is statistically significant at $p=.02$ (or $p<.05$). We reject the null hypothesis that states that there are no differences between the two groups. The likelihood that the decision to reject the null hypothesis is the wrong decision is 2%. The results of the survey show that the majority of the parents (63%) support inclusion while the opinions of the teachers are almost evenly divided (52% oppose and 48% support).

(12.17) a. A *goodness of fit* chi square test for one variable with *unequal* expected frequencies. The responses of those with children are viewed as the sample, and they are compared to a larger population (the expected frequencies) that contains *all* the respondents.

b. The null hypothesis stated that there are no differences between the responses of city residents without school-age children and the responses obtained for the population at large.

c. We retain the null hypothesis. Although the responses of the two groups are not exactly the same, the observed differences are probably due to chance alone and not because of real differences in opinions between the groups.

(12.18) a. A *goodness of fit* chi square test with equal expected frequencies, because there is one independent variable (colors of balls) and we expect all the balls to be equally chosen.

b. The expected frequencies are 10; (Explanation: To find the expected frequencies, divide the number of boys [which is 50] by 5 [the number of colors in the study].)

c. The table reveals that there are differences in color preferences; black and blue are the most popular colors, followed closely by red; green is the least popular color. While the differences between the 5 colors *seem* quite large, they are not *statistically significant* and could have happened by chance more than 5% of the time. The obtained chi square value of 8.800 is lower than the appropriate critical value of 9.488 (at the *p*=.05 level). Therefore, we *retain* the null hypothesis. (Actually, according to the computer printout, the exact *p* value is .07 [which is close to *p*=.05]. With a larger sample size it is likely that there would be statistically significant differences in the color choices.)

(12.19) Even though a higher percentage of elementary-school boys reported that they are happy with the way they are, compared with elementary-school girls, the difference between the genders is not *statistically significant*. The chi square value is quite small (χ^2=0.39) and the *p* value is high (*p*=.53). In general, fewer high-school boys and girls like themselves the way they are compared with elementary-school boys and girls. Just like in elementary school, high-school *boys* like themselves more than do *girls*. However, the difference between the responses of the two genders is higher in high school compared with elementary school. That difference is statistically significant at *p*=.03.

Chapter 13

RELIABILITY

Fill in the blanks:

13.1. When we use a reliable instrument over and over, we expect to get the same _____ each time we use that instrument.

13.2. The consistency of scores obtained for the same group of people upon repeated measures is an indication of the instrument's _____.

13.3. To assess the test-retest reliability of an instrument, the statistical test of _____ is used.

13.4. The two components that make up an *observed* score are the *true* score and a(n) _____ score.

13.5. One way to assess a test reliability is to _____ two alternate forms of the test with each other.

13.6. The Spearman Brown Prophecy formula is used to calculate the reliability of a full-length test by first calculating the _____ between the two split halves.

13.7. When a person has a score of 85 and the test has a standard error of estimate (SEM) of 5, it means that 68% of the time the person's true score is expected to be between the scores of _____ and _____.

Circle the <u>correct</u> answer:

13.8. Instruments measuring human behavior tend to be **more/less** reliable than those measuring physical characteristics.

13.9. The reliability of achievement tests is likely to be **higher/lower** than that of tests measuring attitudes and opinions.

13.10. The test's reliability is likely to *increase* when the test's error component is **increased/decreased**.

13.11. One way to *increase* the test's reliability is to **increase/decrease** the number of items in the test.

13.12. An instrument is administered twice to the same group of people and the correlation between the two set of scores is used to assess the reliability of the test. The reliability would be *higher* when the time interval between the two testing sessions is **shorter/longer**.

13.13. The correlation between two split halves of a test is likely to be **higher/lower** than the correlation between two alternate forms of the same test.

13.14. To assess the reliability of a test using *internal consistency* methods, the test is administered **one time/multiple times**.

13.15. To assess the inter-scorer reliability of an essay, the degree of **agreement/differences** between people who score the same essay is commonly used.

13.16. The higher the reliability, the **lower/higher** the standard error of measurement (SEM).

13.17. When a student takes a norm-referenced test, we can expect that the student's *observed* score would be within ±1SEM **68%/95%** of the time

13.18. When the items on a test are *too easy* or *too difficult*, the test's reliability is likely to **increase/decrease**.

13.19. Teacher-made tests are likely to be **more/less** reliable than commercially produced tests.

13.20. The reliability of tests used for decisions about individual students should be **higher/lower** than the reliability of tests used for group decisions.

Answers - Chapter 13:

(13.1) results, scores;

(13.2) reliability;

(13.3) correlation (or Pearson Product Moment correlation);

(13.4) error;

(13.5) correlate;

(13.6) correlation;

(13.7) 80 and 90; (<u>Explanation</u>: The range of true scores is ±1SEM of the observed score of 85. To find the range of expected true scores, subtract 1SEM from the student's observed score [85-5=80] and add 1SEM to the observed score [85+5=90].)

(13.8) less; (<u>Explanation</u>: Physical characteristics tend to be more stable than human behavior.)

(13.9) higher; (<u>Explanation</u>: Tests that measure achievement provide more consistent and stable information; therefore, they are more reliable than tests that measure attitudes and behavior that tend to fluctuate.)

(13.10) decreased; (<u>Explanation</u>: Tests with a smaller error components are likely to be more reliable.)

(13.11) increase. (<u>Explanation</u>: All things being equal, a longer test is more reliable than a shorter test.)

(13.12) shorter; (<u>Explanation</u>: With longer time intervals between testings, people are more likely to change, and to forget or learn new information.)

(13.13) lower; (<u>Explanation</u>: The two half tests are likely to be shorter than the full-length alternate forms. Therefore, the correlation between the two half tests is likely to be lower. See also the explanation provided for question 13.11 above.)

(13.14) one time; (<u>Explanation</u>: Unlike most other approaches to assess reliability, internal consistency methods can be applied using scores from a single testing.)

(13.15) agreement; (<u>Explanation</u>: The degree [or percent] of agreement between scorers or raters is used as an index of reliability.)

(13.16) lower; (<u>Explanation</u>: The standard error of measurement [SEM] is an index of the level of *error* in a test; therefore, a more reliable test has a smaller level of error.)

(13.17) 68%; (<u>Explanation</u>: As can be seen by the normal curve, 68% of the scores are within ±1SEM of the student's observed score.)

(13.18) decrease; (<u>Explanation</u>: Tests are most reliable when the items have an average level of difficulty.)

(13.19) less; (<u>Explanation</u>: Teachers do not have the expertise or the time necessary to design quality tests whereas commercially produced tests are written by professionals and undergo extensive review and analysis prior to being administered on a large scale.)

(13.20) higher; (<u>Explanation</u>: The stakes are higher when decisions are made about individuals; therefore, tests that are used to assess individuals should be more reliable than tests used for group decisions.)

Chapter 14

VALIDITY

Circle the best answer:

14.1.   Correlation may be used to assess the _____ validity of a test.

      a.   face
      b.   content
      c.   criterion-related

14.2.   A high correlation of a newly developed instrument with another well-established instrument *measuring the same thing* indicates a high _____ validity.

      a.   content
      b.   concurrent
      c.   face

14.3.   The type of validity that is most important for achievement tests is the _____ validity.

      a.   face
      b.   content
      c.   construct

14.4.   The type of validity that is most important for measuring psychological traits is the _____ validity.

      a.   construct
      b.   content
      c.   predictive

Circle the correct answer:

14.5.   Most tests are valid for **a single/multiple** purpose(s).

14.6.   When there is a poor match between course content and a test that is used to assess students in the course, the test is likely to have a **high/low** content validity.

14.7.   Achievement tests written by experienced teachers for their own classrooms tend to have **higher/lower** content validity than commercial tests that are designed to be used nationally in a variety of classrooms.

14.8.   Well-defined instructional objectives may help teachers write tests that have high **content/construct** validity.

14.9.   Administering two instruments to the same group of people within a short time is done to establish the instrument's **predictive/concurrent** validity.

Fill in the blanks:

14.10.   In studies conducted to assess how well the GRE (Graduate Record Examination) predicts graduate school GPA (grade point average), the GRE is considered the _____ variable and the GPA is the _____ variable.

14.11.   To establish the *concurrent* validity of a newly-developed instrument, we can _____ it with a well-established instrument which measures the same thing.

14.12.   Correlating the scores from a newly-developed short version of a personality inventory with a similar full-length personality inventory may be used to establish the _____ validity of the short-version inventory.

14.13.   When a test simply *appears* to measure what it is intended to measure, we conclude that the test has a high _____ validity.

14.14.   In assessing the instrument's criterion-related validity, the relationship between the instrument and the criterion is indicated by the _____ coefficient.

14.15.   When a test systematically discriminates against a group of test-takers, the test is considered _____.

Answers - Chapter 14:

(14.1) c;

(14.2) b;

(14.3) b;

(14.4) a;

(14.5) a single;

(14.6) low;

(14.7) higher; (<u>Explanation</u>: Teachers can write items that more closely match what they have taught in class.)

(14.8) content; (<u>Explanation</u>; Well-defined objectives help guide the teachers by listing the content of the materials taught in class. Teachers can then write test items that correspond to the objectives.)

(14.9) concurrent;

(14.10) predictor; criterion (or *predicted*);

(14.11) correlate;

(14.12) concurrent;

(14.13) face;

(14.14) validity (or *correlation*);

(14.15) biased;

Chapter 15

PLANNING AND CONDUCTING RESEARCH STUDIES

Circle the <u>correct</u> answer:

15.1.   Research plans for *quantitative* studies are usually **more/less** detailed compared with plans for *qualitative* studies.

15.2.   After a study has started, its participants **<u>should/should not</u>** be allowed to withdraw from the study.

15.3.   When teachers conduct action research in their own classrooms with students they know well, they **<u>should/should not</u>** be concerned about ethical issues.

15.4.   The most popular writing style used by students writing research papers is the one which was developed by the **<u>Modern Language Association/American Psychological Association</u>**.

15.5.   A description of how the sample that was used in the study was selected is likely to be found in the **<u>Methodology/Literature Review</u>** chapter.

15.6.   Opinions that contradict those of the researcher writing the research report **<u>should/should not</u>** be included in the report.

15.7.   <u>Detailed</u> information about a standardized test that were used in a study, such as its norms, reliability, and validity, is likely to be found in the **<u>Abstract/Methodology chapter</u>**.

15.8.   A very *brief* description of how the present study was conducted is likely to be found in the **<u>Methodology chapter/Abstract</u>**.

15.9.   Proposals are usually written in **<u>past/present/future</u>** tense.

15.10. Research reports are usually written in **<u>past/present/future</u>** tense.

15.11. The literature reviews in research *reports* tend to be **<u>shorter/longer</u>** than in research *proposals*.

Circle the best answer:

15.12. Which of the following is NOT included in research proposals?

    a.   The study's results.
    b.   The study's methodology.
    c.   A review of literature related to the study.
    d.   Introduction.

15.13. Which document may be viewed as a blueprint for the planned study?

    a.   Discussion.
    b.   Proposal.
    c.   Abstract.
    d.   Literature Review.

15.14. The most comprehensive rationale for the study is likely to be found in the _____ chapter.

    a.   Methodology
    b.   Results
    c.   Introduction
    d.   Literature Review

15.15 The most comprehensive statement of the problem to be investigated in the study is usually found in the study's _____

    a.   Instrumentation section.
    b.   Literature Review chapter.
    c.   Procedure section.
    d.   Introduction.

15.16. When writing a literature review, it should be organized _____

    a.   in chronological order.
    b.   by topics and subtopics.
    c.   as an annotated bibliography.
    d.   from the most to the least related references.

15.17. The statistical findings of the study are presented in detail in the _____

    a.   Abstract.
    b.   Methodology chapter.
    c.   Introduction chapter.
    d.   Results chapter.

15.18. Most of the background information, such as summaries of other studies related to the present study, is reported in the study's _____

    a.   Literature Review.
    b.   Methodology.
    c.   Procedure.
    d.   Abstract.

15.19. An explanation of some possible reasons why the results of a study that is described in the research report have not confirmed its hypothesis is found in the _____

    a.   study's proposal.
    b.   Methodology chapter.
    c.   Results chapter.
    d.   Discussion chapter.

15.20. In a report on an experimental study, a *detailed* description of the intervention is likely to be found in the _____ section of the *Methodology* chapter.

    a.   Instrument
    b.   Sample
    c.   Procedure
    d.   Data Analysis

Chapter 15: Answers

(15.1) more;

(15.2) should; (<u>Explanation</u>: All participants, in all types of studies, should be allowed to withdraw from the study at any time.)

(15.3) should; (<u>Explanation</u>: All researchers, including teachers who study their own classrooms, should be concerned about issues of ethics.)

(15.4) American Psychological Association;

(15.5) Methodology;

(15.6) should;

(15.7) Methodology section; (<u>Explanation</u>: While some brief information about an instrument used in the study may be found in the *Abstract*, detailed information is likely to be found in the study's *Methodology*.)

(15.8) Abstract; (<u>Explanation</u>: Because the *Abstract* is usually limited in length, it can contain only brief information about the study.)

(15.9) future; (<u>Explanation</u>: The proposal describes the plans of the researcher.)

(15.10) past; (<u>Explanation</u>: The report describes a study that has been concluded; therefore, *past* tense should be used.)

(15.11) longer;

(15.12) a; (<u>Explanation</u>: Proposals are written before the study is conducted; therefore, they do not report the study's results. *Methodology, Literature Review*, and *Introduction* can be found in both proposals and research reports.)

(15.13) b;

(15.14) c;

(15.15) d;

(15.16) b;

(15.17) d; (<u>Explanation</u>: While the *Abstract* is likely to summarize briefly the study's results, a comprehensive description of the results are found in the *Results* chapter.)

(15.18) a; (<u>Explanation</u>: One of the main goals of the *Literature Review* is to provide background information about the topic of the study.)

(15.19) d; (<u>Explanation</u>: Explanations of the study's findings and interpretations of the results are found in the *Discussion* chapter.)

(15.20) c;